Independent Schools
Examinations Board

ENGLISH
ISEB Revision Guide
2nd Edition

Susan Elkin

Editor: Tom Cross

Independent Schools
Examinations Board

www.galorepark.co.uk

GALORE PARK

Published by ISEB Publications, an imprint of Galore Park Publishing
19/21 Sayers Lane, Tenterden, Kent TN30 6BW
www.galorepark.co.uk

Text copyright © Susan Elkin Ltd 2013

The right of Susan Elkin to be identified as the author of this work has been asserted by her in accordance with sections 77 and 78 of Copyright, Designs and Patents Act 1988.

Typesetting by Typetechnique

Printed by Charlesworth Press, Wakefield

ISBN: 978 1 907047 86 2

All rights reserved: no part of this publication may be reproduced, stored ina retrieval system, or transmitted in any form or by any means, electronic, mechanical, photocopying, recording or otherwise, without either the prior written permission of the copyright owner or a licence permitting restricted copying issued by the Copyright Licensing Agency, Saffron House, 6–10 Kirby Street, London EC1N 8TS.

First edition published 2008, second edition published 2013

Details of other ISEB Revision Guides for Common Entrance, examination papers and Galore Park publications are available at www.galorepark.co.uk

Front cover illustration: © Mary Evans Picture Library/Alamy. Peter Pan and Wendy fly over the rooftops in a poster to advertise the stage show.

The publishers are grateful for permission to reproduce the following extracts:

Anita and Me by Meera Syal, permission sought. *The Day of the Triffids* by John Wyndham, published by Penguin © The Estate of John Wyndham. *Under the Tuscan Sun* by Frances Mayes, published by Curtis Brown, permission sought. Playscript of *War Horse* by Nick Stafford based on the novel by Michael Morpugo, published by Faber and Faber Ltd. 'Delusions of Grandeur' by Susan Elkin, published by *The Independent.*

Contents

Introduction

This book leads the student, teacher and parent through the preparation for the Common Entrance 13+ exam in English set by the Independent Schools Examinations Board.

It can, of course, be used independently by the student. It is also designed to help teachers leading revision in a classroom by providing advice and information to share, along with plenty of sample tasks to practise. Equally there is a great deal here to support the parent helping his or her child at home.

Revision can be dull. But it need not be. Everything in this book is as fresh and exciting as I know how to make it. English, with all those fantastic words, books and ideas, is a great joy.

Preparing for an exam in English should enhance pleasure in the subject not diminish it.

Happy revising!

Susan Elkin July 2013

A note to parents

It may be a very long time since you studied English yourself. Perhaps you have forgotten some of the finer points. I sympathise. I'm afraid I have 'lost' most of the maths I must once have known and I find my ignorance quite embarrassing sometimes.

Chapter 6 of this book offers a very quick guide to grammar, punctuation and spelling, and there's much more, in greater detail, in my *So you really want to learn English* books.

If, however, you still feel you're on shaky ground and want to boost your confidence, I recommend *Grammar for Grown Ups* by Katherine Fry and Rowena Kirton, published by Square Peg, 2012.

Susan Elkin

Chapter 1: Approaching the exam

1.1 How to use this book

This is not a textbook. It is a revision book to help you in the last few months and weeks before you take your senior school entrance exams in Year 8 at 13+.

Its purpose is to remind you of all you have learnt in English lessons and to show you how to write good answers.

Probably, by now, you have already done quite a lot of work from textbooks. This will have widened your knowledge and understanding of English – such a lovely subject with all those delicious words and opportunities to read extensively.

Revision – which comes from Latin and means 'looking again' – is just that. You need to spend time looking back at all you have learnt so that you can show the examiner just how much you now understand, know and can do.

There are no facts to memorise in English. It is different from subjects like history, geography or science. The exam tests your ability to read perceptively, and to write well and accurately. It examines the skills which you have developed through class work.

This book builds on everything you have learnt until now and shows you how to do your best in the exam. It also provides quick reminders of the grammar, punctuation and spelling you have already been taught, as well as the technical terms you need when you are writing about English literature.

Your 13+ English exam will involve two papers and four tasks. In this book we cover first the reading tasks, then the writing tasks. The exam presents the papers and tasks as outlined in the syllabus over the page.

> **TOP TIP**
> This is a good time to sort out all those little grammar points that you still make mistakes with such as when to use 'its' and 'it's' or how to use 'me' and 'I' correctly. There is help with this in Chapter 6.

> **TOP TIP**
> As you work through the chapters – if this is your own copy of the book – you might find it helpful and encouraging to tick off the sections as you complete them. You can also make notes in the book, if you find this useful, or you can keep a revision notebook to chart your learning.

1.2 The syllabus and your exams

Your teacher will have told you what your exams involve. But, to ensure that you are quite clear about it, look carefully at this summary so that you know exactly what you will be asked to do.

Paper 1:

Section A: Comprehension exercise on a passage from a novel, a play, a(n) (auto)biography or a piece of travel writing

AND

Section B: An essay on a non-fiction topic. There are at least five questions to choose from, two of which will ask you to write about a book or books you have read.

(1 hour 15 minutes, which includes planning time, 50 marks: 25 marks for Section A and 25 marks for Section B)

Paper 2:

Section A: Comprehension exercise on a poem

AND

Section B: An imaginative, descriptive or narrative composition – a story, for example, on a subject you choose from at least four options on the paper.

(1 hour 15 minutes, which includes planning time, 50 marks: 25 marks for Section A and 25 marks for Section B)

Levels 1 and 2

Both 13+ Common Entrance papers are offered at two levels. Level 1 is a foundation level and Level 2 is a standard level.

Both papers will use the same passage or poem for comprehension but:

- at Level 1 the passage may be abridged so that it's slightly shorter and more difficult words may be explained
- the questions are different at each level. Level 1 questions offer the candidate more guidance than Level 2 questions.

The writing tasks on both papers are the same for each level.

In this book we give examples of comprehension passage questions at both levels and show you ways of tackling them.

What are the examiners looking for?

The people marking your papers hope to see three main things. They want to see that you can:

- read substantial passages unaided and give independent written responses to questions requiring a range of comprehension skills
- write original creative work in the limited time the exam allows you
- use language for practical purposes, which may include responding to books you've read on your own or in class.

It is a good idea to keep these three things in mind as you revise and even while you are writing your exam answers.

1.3 How to revise

Find a quiet place in which to revise. Few of us can do our best work and thinking when there is a lot of distracting background noise.

Organise your revision so that you do at least half an hour every second day. If you revise some English for a short time regularly you will probably have worked pretty thoroughly through what you need to know.

> **TOP TIP**
> At home, use your bedroom or some other peaceful spot for revision. At school, the library may be best.

Don't try to revise the whole of one subject before you move on to another. That way some subjects are bound to get left too late and have to be hurried. You might also have forgotten, by exam time, some of the work you did at the beginning. Aim to keep all your subjects evenly 'on the boil'.

Don't force yourself to work for hours without a break. Stop for five minutes at least once every half hour. Research about how people learn has shown that most people absorb more if they do this. Spend your break usefully – some physical exercise is particularly good for refreshing the brain with oxygen.

Promise yourself a little treat when the exams are over and you can stop revising – perhaps an exciting book which you have been looking forward to reading or a DVD you want to watch. This helps to put you in a better frame of mind for revision.

Use past papers to familiarise yourself with the format of the exam. You will feel much more confident going into the exam if you know what to expect.

Do some physical activity every day during your revision. You will not be able to revise effectively if you are not feeling fit and well.

Eat healthy food while you are revising and don't skip meals. Your brain works better when you give it good fuel.

> **TOP TIP**
> Make the most of all the expertise and talent available to you in school. If you really don't understand something, it's sometimes worth asking a teacher other than your own. Every teacher has his or her own way of explaining things and we all learn in different ways. You may find that suddenly you understand something which has always given you trouble.

Make sure you read as many books as you can while you are revising to improve your own personal word bank.

If you are planning in Paper 1 to write about a text you have read, then make sure you re-read the two or three books you have studied recently, and think which you might want to write about in the exam. Remind yourself of any written work you have done on them or of notes you have made.

As you revise, practise writing paragraphs consisting of sentences of different lengths and different shapes. Notice and think about sentence length and shape while you're reading too.

Find some suitable passages from books and other places and devise your own sample papers. Then write the sort of questions based on them which you think an examiner would ask. Practise writing answers to your own questions – or swap with someone else.

TOP TIP
As part of your revision, make lists of words which have more than one meaning, and useful verbs for analytical or non-fiction writing.

1.4 How to tackle the exam

Try to get a good night's sleep the night before the exam. You will be able to approach the exam much more positively if you feel refreshed. Don't eat too late the night before and have a good breakfast in the morning.

Check that you have everything you need to take into the exam. Take at least two pens in case one runs out. Your teacher will tell you if there are any other items you need to take as well.

If your school allows it, take some water into the exam with you.

Make sure you read and understand the rubric (instructions and rules) on the front of the exam paper.

Read the exam passage(s) right through carefully.

Look closely at the sentence at the top of the passage which introduces it. It's there to help you.

If the meanings of any of the words in the passage(s) are given at the bottom to help you, make sure you refer to these as you read.

Read all the questions you are asked to answer, at least twice.

Never begin to write your answers before you have read the passage(s) and the questions thoroughly.

TOP TIP
Allow some time at the start to read and consider the questions carefully before writing anything. Don't rush into answering before you have had a chance to think about it.

Manage your time and check your work

Making the best use of your time is one of the most important things to get right in an exam. It can make a big difference to your marks.

For Section A allow 5 minutes to read the passage or poem and make notes. Then split the time into little blocks for each question (some answers will be shorter than others). Allow more time for a question carrying, for example, 5 or 6 marks than for a short 2-mark question. Try not to over-run on one question, leaving too little time for another. Spend no more than 25 minutes on your comprehension answers. Then spend 5 minutes checking your work.

For Section B allow 5 minutes to read the writing tasks and plan your answer. Then spend 25 minutes writing your essay. Then spend 5 minutes checking your work.

You **must** leave a few minutes at the end to double check the whole of your paper. Correct any obvious spelling mistakes. Make sure every sentence ends with a full stop. Put in any words you may have left out. Sort out any other slips you can spot. Make quick improvements where you can.

Remember to keep an eye on the clock in the room. If you don't spread your time properly across all the questions, don't finish or manage to check your work before you hand in your paper you have not shown the examiner what you can really do.

> **TOP TIP**
>
> For more tips on how to get the best from your revision and exams, see *Study Skills* by Elizabeth Holtom, published by Galore Park.

1.5 Useful resources

Study Skills by Elizabeth Holtom, ISBN: 978 1 902984 59 9

So you really want to learn English Book 2 by Susan Elkin, ISBN: 978 1 905735 62 4, second edition, 2012

So you really want to learn English Book 2 Answer Book by Susan Elkin, ISBN: 978 1 905735 68 6, second edition, 2012

So you really want to learn English Book 3 by Susan Elkin, ISBN: 978 1 905735 63 1, second edition, 2012

So you really want to learn English Book 3 Answer Book by Susan Elkin, ISBN: 978 1 905735 69 3, second edition, 2012

All available from Galore Park: www.galorepark.co.uk

Chapter 2: Literary prose comprehension

In this chapter we will look at the type of passage you are required to read and respond to in Paper 1 and suggest ways in which you might tackle the task. At the end of the chapter there is a full-length exam question for you to practise on.

The first section of Paper 1 requires you to read a passage, or sometimes two short extracts, from a novel, play, biography, autobiography or piece of travel writing and answer questions on it.

It is your opportunity to show the examiner that you:

- can read with understanding and have a good vocabulary
- can use what you have read to illustrate your answers
- can work out what a writer is implying but not saying directly
- are able to comment on style and a writer's use of language
- can give an opinion, make a judgement or construct an argument based on what you have read
- are aware how grammar, word order and punctuation can affect meaning in writing
- can spot and explain comparisons and contrasts when you meet them in writing.

> **TOP TIP**
> Remember that in English comprehension work there are often no right or wrong answers. The main thing is that you can justify your answers.

There may be several ways of answering a question in your own words. It is your opportunity to show what and how you think. You might even spot something examiners haven't thought of. Even if it is not exactly what the examiner has written on his or her mark sheet, you will get good marks for writing something sensible and thoughtful – as long as it answers the question and you can back up what you say with evidence from the text.

2.1 Getting the basics right

Read the passage

It may sound obvious, but the first and most important thing you have to do is to read the passage through carefully. Of course, the advice here also applies to the poetry in Paper 2.

Some people find it helps to subvocalise. This means you read the passage aloud to yourself in your head slowly – rather than reading it fast as if it were a story you were reading casually for fun at home. Others prefer to skim-read it once and then read it a second time, more slowly. Most people find it useful to read the passage more than once. Decide which method works best for you.

Look closely at the sentence at the top of the page which introduces the passage. It's there to help you.

If the meanings of any of the words in the passage are given at the bottom, make sure you refer to these as you read.

Read the questions

Read all the questions you are asked to answer, at least twice. Think about what they mean and make notes if you wish.

Never begin to write your answers before you have read both the passage and the questions thoroughly. You might like to highlight key words in the questions and the text as you read.

Use the right style in your answers

Answer most questions in full sentences. It is usually incorrect to begin a sentence with 'because' or words like 'plus'.

Use a capital letter at the beginning and a full stop at the end of each whole sentence. If your answer needs other punctuation such as commas, then be careful where you place them.

If you are asked for short details or points from a passage (for example, you are asked to give another word for one that is in the passage to show that you understand it), then you need not use a whole sentence.

You must stick closely to the information given in the passage in your answers but use your own words as much as you can.

Take great care with spelling. It is particularly careless to misspell a word which is in the passage or questions.

Be as precise as you can.

Answer as fully as you can

Put as much detail into your answers as you can. A good answer may need several sentences.

Highlight key words

If you are asked to summarise information from the passage, highlight the key words in the passage.

Then sum up whatever points you are asked about in your own words, quoting short phrases to make sure that your answer stays close to the passage. Do not put these phrases on separate lines. Weave them into your sentences and put inverted commas around them.

Don't forget that the purpose of all this is for you to show that you have understood the passage.

> **TOP TIP**
> The whole reading process can take several minutes. Do not panic if the person next to you begins writing immediately. Your answers will probably be better than his or hers because you have read and thought carefully before writing them.

> **TOP TIP**
> Avoid slang and sloppy expressions such as 'like' (unless you mean similar to), 'cool' (unless you mean at a low-ish temperature) and *never* write 'and stuff'.

Use evidence from the passage

You must be able to prove, or back up, every answer with evidence from the passage. This is important, so:

- refer in your own words to what the writer says

- quote single words and short phrases (with inverted commas around them) woven into your answers

- look for, and comment on, parts of the passage in which the writer hints at something, but perhaps doesn't, for some reason, say it straightforwardly. In other words, ask yourself what lies under or behind the writer's words. You may have been taught to call this the 'subtext'.

> **TOP TIP**
> Remember you are like a scientist. Look in the passage for evidence to 'prove' what you write.

2.2 Different types of writing

The passage(s) you are set to read can be fiction or non-fiction and will be one of the following:

- part of a novel or short story (look for characters, dialogue, imaginative description and sometimes a storyteller who is part of the story)

- part of a real-life story – a biography or autobiography (watch for the writer looking back at, or describing, personal events which happened in the past)

- a passage taken from a travel book – an account of the writer's experiences at a place he or she has visited or lived in (be prepared to write about the author's thoughts and feelings about the place and his or her use of language)

- an extract from a play (be aware of what you learn about the characters from what they say and do and notice how the playwright uses stage directions).

2.3 Sample questions and answers

Try these yourself, covering up the sample answer. Then, when you've written your own response, compare it with the one given here.

Remember, though, that there are very few absolutely right or absolutely wrong answers in English. The answers given here are just suggestions as to how you might respond. The important thing is for you to be able to back-up your answer with evidence from the passage.

Sample 1 (Autobiography)

Look at the following sentence about South American screamer birds.

All we knew was that screamers were supposed to be entirely vegetarian, but whenever a butterfly hovered within six feet of Egbert, his whole being seemed to be filled with blood-lust, his eyes would take on a fanatical and most un-vegetarian-like gleam and he would endeavour to stalk it.

(From *The Drunken Forest* by Gerald Durrell, 1956)

Level 1 question

What do you learn about screamer birds from this sentence? (2 marks)

Answer

Screamer birds do not eat meat. They eat only plant foods. The writer notices, though, that Egbert likes to chase butterflies and try to catch them which he thinks is funny. In expressions such as 'blood-lust' and 'un-vegetarian-like gleam' he is using hyperbole to convey his amusement. The bird cannot possibly be reasoning and acting contrary to its nature as he pretends to think. It's simply a witty way of describing the young bird's fascination with things which move.

Level 2 question

What amuses the writer about screamer birds? (2 marks)

Answer

Although screamer birds are plant eaters, this particular one ('Egbert') seems strangely interested in watching and trying to catch butterflies. The writer is intrigued because such determination and the intent look in the bird's eyes humorously suggest that it is hard to believe it does not regard the butterfly as prey.

TOP TIP

Look at the number of marks given after each question on the exam paper. This is a guide as to how much you should write in your answers.

Sample 2 (Fiction)

The narrator is walking through a wood towards a mysterious house.

Darkness swallowed me; the branches arched high overhead; I saw only glimpses of the paler sky through their tracery. My feet crunched beech mast. I smelled the coolness of the mossy earth and heard the trickle of water close by. As my eyes accustomed themselves to dimmer light, I saw that here, on the lower ground, a faint mist hung in the air, trapped perhaps beneath the trees. I must be careful not to stray from the path, which I could only dimly discern; but before many minutes had passed, wrought iron gates reared ahead of me, set in a wall of flint. Though I had reached the edge of the wood my way was barred. The gate, must, however, be unlocked, as my arrival was expected.

(From *Set in Stone* by Linda Newbery, 2006)

Level 1 question

Sum up the narrator's thoughts and impressions as he approaches the gates. (4 marks)

Answer

All the narrator's senses are aroused by the dark, mysterious wood he is passing through at dusk on his way to gates leading to a property where he is an expected visitor. He hears 'crunched beech mast' under his feet and the sound of water nearby. He smells 'mossy earth' and can see trees, mist and, eventually, the big, rather sinister ('reared') gates in front of him. He seems to be nervous because he is in a place which is new to him. That is why he is alert to every sensation around him.

Level 2 question

How does the writer create a sense of anticipation as the narrator approaches the gates? (4 marks)

Answer

The writer writes very sensually. All the narrator's senses are aroused by the dark, mysterious wood he is passing through at dusk on his way to gates leading to a property where he is an expected visitor. He hears 'crunched beech mast' under his feet and the sound of water nearby. He smells 'mossy earth' and can see trees, mist and, eventually, the big, rather sinister ('reared') gates in front of him. The writer evokes fear of the unfamiliar and a sense of unease by using short, quite jerky statements linked by semi-colons in the first sentence.

TOP TIP

In fiction, look at what characters say and at what the narrator says.

Sample 3 (Fiction)

Jody follows the trail of his dying pony and finds buzzards with its body.

Jody leaped forward and plunged down the hill. The wet ground muffled his steps and the brush hid him. When he arrived it was all over. The first buzzard sat on the pony's head. Jody plunged into the circle like a cat. The black brotherhood rose in a cloud, but the big one on the pony's head was too late. As it hopped along to take off, Jody caught its wing tip and pulled it down. It was nearly as big as he was. The free wing crashed into his face with the force of a club but he hung on. The claws fastened on his leg and the wing elbows battered his head on either side. Jody groped wildly with his free hand; his fingers found the neck of the struggling bird. The red eyes looked into his face, calm and fearless and fierce: he held the bird's neck to the ground with one hand while with the other he found a piece of sharp white quartz. He struck again and again until the buzzard lay dead. He was still beating the dead bird when Billy Buck pulled him off and held him to calm his shaking.

(Slightly abridged from *The Red Pony* by John Steinbeck, 1937)

Level 1 question

Why does Jody kill the buzzard? (4 marks)

Answer

Jody is upset because his pony has died. Jody had 'leaped' and 'plunged' in his hurry, but the animal is already dead, so he is also cross with himself. Buzzards feed on freshly dead flesh and a group – looking sinister and greedy ('black brotherhood') – has been waiting for the pony to die. Jody attacks the big bird. He is not thinking rationally. The writer tells us that Jody 'groped wildly' and then he goes on hitting the struggling bird with a piece of rock even after it is dead. This is the action of a boy who is frustrated and angry and wanting – or needing – to take his feelings out on something.

Level 2 question

What can you deduce about Jody's reasons for killing the buzzard? (6 marks)

Answer

Jody is beside himself with rage and distress because his pony has died and because, although he 'leaped' and 'plunged' in his hurry, he is too late to see the animal's last moments. Buzzards feed on freshly dead flesh and a group – looking sinister and greedy ('black brotherhood') – has been waiting near the dying, now dead, pony. Although he is quite young – the bird is not much smaller than he is – Jody launches a frenzied attack on the bird which has already perched on the pony's head ready to feed. He is not thinking rationally. The writer tells us that Jody 'groped wildly' and then he goes on hitting the bird with a piece of rock even after it is dead. He is probably full of adrenaline and extra strength because he is so upset and angry about his pony's death. He manages to hold onto the big bird despite its struggling and kills it even though it claws his leg and tries to beat him off with its strong wings. This is presented as the action of a boy who is frustrated and angry and wanting – or needing – to take his feelings out on something. If he lives in the country he must know that the buzzards don't kill ponies.

TOP TIP

A full answer will make good use of evidence from the passage.

Sample 4 (Drama)

Buddy's father Terry has broken the law but now wants an honest job.

Buddy	*Dad…*
Terry	*You do two things. Buddy Clark: cry or say you're sorry, and you're out that door. Right?* (Buddy struggles not to cry but as his face screws up, Terry cuts in)
Terry	*I didn't 'ear you say 'Yes'.*
Buddy	*Yes.*
Terry	*And there's another fing before your mum starts in about where you bin. It might be six months before me trial comes up in court and I've promised 'er I'll get a job. You said them black friends – they still looking for drivers?* (Buddy runs to Terry and crushes himself against his chest. Carol closes the front door)

(From the TV script of *Buddy* by Nigel Hinton, 1987)

Level 1 question

What does this extract tell you about Terry and Buddy? (4 marks)

Answer

Terry and Buddy are father and son. Terry speaks with an accent and says 'fing' and 'bin'. We know that Buddy has just arrived home after an unexplained absence because Terry tells Buddy that his mother will want to talk to him about where he's been. Buddy is struggling not to cry because he is pleased to see his father with whom he seems to have had a row. Both are trying to be brave. We learn that Terry has broken the law: 'It might be six months before me trial comes up.' Meanwhile he tells Buddy that he wants to get an honest job. At the end Buddy hugs Terry to show that they love and have forgiven each other.

TOP TIP

In drama, look closely at the stage directions as well as what the characters say.

How does the playwright convey the relationship between Terry and Buddy in this extract? (5 marks)

Answer

The playwright shows us Buddy, clearly distressed ('struggles not to cry') but having a reconciliation with his father Terry. The front door is open (Carol doesn't close it until the end of the passage) and we infer that Buddy has just arrived home after an unexplained absence because Terry tells Buddy that his mother will want to talk to him about where he's been. Both are trying to be brave. Terry has broken the law: 'It might be six months before me trial comes up.' Meanwhile he is trying to reassure Buddy by telling him that he means to get an honest job. The playwright makes Terry speak with an accent and shows it in the script by spelling words such as 'fing' and 'bin' phonetically. It is probably an attempt by the playwright to make Terry sound natural and sincere as he makes his peace with Buddy. When Buddy hugs Terry wordlessly the playwright wants us to understand that they love and have forgiven each other. At the end of this passage Carol closes the front door. Dramatically that makes it clear that Buddy and Terry are together inside the house.

Sample 5 (Travel writing)

The author describes his natural, open-air bath.

> *Near the house was one of the miracles of El Valero: a torrent of water that rushed out from a rock and tumbled into a little pool below. I sat in the pool and poured bucketful after bucketful over my head and body. There was a soapdish and a bottle of shampoo and towels and some washing hanging from a wire strung between two acacia trees. Without needing to put shoes or clothes on, I could take just five paces and pick oranges, mandarins, figs or grapes, fresh from the trees. I cooled them in the waterfall and stuffed myself.*
>
> (From *Driving Over Lemons* by Chris Stewart, 1999)

Level 1 question

Sum up in your own words what the writer likes about his outdoor shower. (3 marks)

Answer

The waterfall – his shower – is completely natural. The water gushes out of a rock into a pool which he can use as a bath. It is a novelty. The writer also likes being able to pick fruits from trees very close to the shower. The weather seems to be hot. He is quite comfortable naked in the open air and has to cool his fruit before eating it. The waterfall and pool are cool and he enjoys pouring 'bucketful after bucketful' of water over himself.

TOP TIP

As with fiction, in travel writing think about how the writer brings alive the place he or she is describing.

Level 2 question

Why does the writer regard his outdoor shower as 'one of the miracles of El Valero'? (4 marks)

Answer

He is impressed and entranced because the waterfall – which is effectively an outdoor shower – is completely natural. The water gushes out of a rock into a pool which he can use as a bath. And someone has left soap, shampoo and towels for him so showering out of doors is clearly accepted practice at El Valero. The same person has apparently also hung out washing to dry and that adds to the novelty. Second, the writer also marvels at being able to pick fruits from trees very close to the shower and eat them without dressing himself. We infer that it is hot. He is quite comfortable naked in the open air, has to cool his fruit before eating it and the washing is drying in the sunshine. The waterfall and pool provides respite from the heat and sun which adds to his enthusiastic enjoyment ('bucketful after bucketful') of it.

Sample 6 (Autobiography)

It is time for Frank McCourt and his siblings to settle down for the night.

> *Soon we're all in bed and if there's the odd flea I don't mind because it's warm in the bed with the six of us and I love the glow of the fire – the way it dances on the walls and ceiling and makes the room go red and black, red and black, till it dims to white and black and all you can hear is a little cry from Oliver turning in my mother's arms.*

(From *Angela's Ashes* by Frank McCourt, 1996)

Level 1 question

How does the writer feel about going to bed? (3 marks)

Answer

He is so pleased to be cosily ('warm in the bed') tucked up with five other family members that he doesn't even worry about fleas. The fire makes him happy too. 'I love the glow,' he writes. He likes watching it reflected on the ceiling and then gradually going out. Late at night when the fire has died away it is very quiet. He can hear nothing except 'a little cry from Oliver' and the child turning in his mother's arms. It all seems very secure and happy – although they are obviously quite poor if they all have to sleep in the same bed and it's dirty.

TOP TIP

As with all writing, when you read biography or autobiography look closely at details the writer has included and think about what they add.

> **Level 2 question**
>
> What techniques does the writer use to make this description of the children's bedtime vivid? (3 marks)
>
> **Answer**
>
> Although he is looking back as an adult, the writer uses the present tense rather than the past to create a sense that the reader is inside the mind of the child. He writes sensually – telling us how it feels to be in the bed (warm), what he can see (reflections of the fire on the ceiling) and hear (Oliver crying). He uses repetition to suggest the soporific flickering of the fire flames as the room grows quiet and the six children (presumably) fall asleep.

2.4 Practice tasks

Now practise your skills on these tasks which are examples of what you can expect in Paper 1 Section A.

The marks at the end of each question are a guide as to how much you should write in your answers.

You should spend around 35 minutes in total on each task. Spend the first 5 minutes planning. Write for about 25 minutes. Read your work through in the last 5 minutes to check for mistakes and to make small changes.

There are suggestions to show you how to write good answers in Chapter 7. Do not look at these until you've tried each exercise yourself. Then consult the suggestions to see how you might have done it better.

1. Fiction

Level 1

A sudden disaster has struck London. Nearly all its population has been blinded. The narrator is one of the few who can still see.

1   *I crossed in the direction of Piccadilly. I was about to start along it when I noticed a steady tapping not far away, and coming closer. A man, more neatly dressed than any other I had seen that morning, was walking rapidly towards me, hitting the wall beside him with a white stick. As he caught the sound of my steps he stopped, listening alertly.*

5   *'It's all right,' I told him. 'Come on.'*

I felt relieved to see him. He was, so to speak, normally blind. His dark glasses were much less disturbing than the staring but useless eyes of others.

'Stand still, then,' he said. 'I've already been bumped into by God knows how many fools today. Why is it so quiet? I know it isn't night – I can feel the sunlight. What's gone wrong with everything?'

10   *I told him as much as I knew.*

He said nothing for almost a minute. Then he gave a short, bitter laugh.

'There's one thing,' he said. 'They'll be needing all their damned patronage for themselves now.'

With that he straightened up, a little defiantly.

'Thank you. Good luck,' he said to me, and set off westwards wearing an exaggerated air of
15   *independence.*

The sound of his briskly confident tapping gradually died away behind me as I made my way up Piccadilly.

There were no people to be seen now, and I walked among the scatter of stranded vehicles in the road. Out there I was much less disturbing to the people feeling their way along the fronts of the
20   *buildings, for every time they heard a step close by they would stop and brace themselves against a possible collision. Such collisions were taking place all down the street, but there was one I found significant. The subjects of it had been groping along a shop front from opposite directions when they met with a bump. One was a young man wearing a well-cut suit, but wearing a tie obviously selected by touch alone: the other a woman who carried a small child. [...]*

25   *'Wait a minute,' he said. 'Can your child see?'*

'Yes,' she said. 'But I can't.'

The young man turned. He put one finger on the plate-glass window, pointing.

'Look, Sonny, what's in there?' he asked.

'Not Sonny,' the child objected.

30   *'Go on, Mary. Tell the gentleman,' her mother encouraged her.*

'Pretty ladies,' said the child.

The man took the woman by the arm, and felt his way to the next window.

'And what's in here?' he asked again.

'Apples and fings,' the child told him.

35
'Fine!' said the young man.

He pulled off his shoe, and hit the window with a smart smack with the heel of it. The crash reverberated up and down the street. He restored his shoe, put an arm cautiously through the broken window, and felt about until he found a couple of oranges. One he gave to the woman and one to the child. He felt about again, found one for himself, and began to peel it. The woman
40   *fingered hers.*

'But – ' she began.

'What's the matter? Don't like oranges?' he asked.

'This isn't right,' she said. 'We didn't ought to take 'em. Not like this.'

'How else are you going to get food?' he inquired.

(Slightly abridged from *The Day of the Triffids* by John Wyndham, 1951)

1. Look carefully at paragraph 1. Why is the writer surprised? (1)

2. Choose three words or phrases from lines 1–17 which show what impresses the narrator about the man with the white stick. (3)
   Explain your choices. (3)

3. What does the writer want us to know about the young man in the suit in lines 22–44? (4)

4. What do we learn about the woman in lines 22–44? (4)

5. Write two short quotations from any part of the passage which show how quiet London now is. (2)
   Explain your choices. (4)

6. The woman does not want to steal. How does the author make this clear? (4)
   Explain your views.

Level 2

A sudden disaster has struck London. Nearly all its population has been blinded. The narrator is one of the few who can still see.

1 *Still magnetically drawn towards the old centre of things, I crossed in the direction of Piccadilly. I was about to start along it when I noticed a sharp new sound – a steady tapping not far away, and coming closer. Looking up I discovered its source. A man, more neatly dressed than any other I had seen that morning, was walking rapidly towards me, hitting the wall beside him with a white*
5 *stick. As he caught the sound of my steps he stopped, listening alertly.*

'It's all right,' I told him. 'Come on.'

I felt relieved to see him. He was, so to speak, normally blind. His dark glasses were much less disturbing than the staring but useless eyes of others.

'Stand still, then,' he said. 'I've already been bumped into by God knows how many fools today.
10 *What the devil's happened? Why is it so quiet? I know it isn't night – I can feel the sunlight. What's gone wrong with everything?'*

I told him as much as I knew.

When I had finished he said nothing for almost a minute, then he gave a short, bitter laugh.

'There's one thing,' he said. 'They'll be needing all their damned patronage for themselves now.'

15 *With that he straightened up, a little defiantly.*

'Thank you. Good luck,' he said to me, and set off westwards wearing an exaggerated air of independence.

The sound of his briskly confident tapping gradually died away behind me as I made my way up Piccadilly.

20　*There were no people to be seen now, and I walked among the scatter of stranded vehicles in the road. Out there I was much less disturbing to the people feeling their way along the fronts of the buildings, for every time they heard a step close by they would stop and brace themselves against a possible collision. Such collisions were taking place every now and then all down the street, but there was one I found significant. The subjects of it had been groping along a shop front from*

25　*opposite directions when they met with a bump. One was a young man wearing a well-cut suit, but wearing a tie obviously selected by touch alone: the other a woman who carried a small child. The child whined something inaudible. The young man had started to edge his way past the woman. He stopped abruptly.*

'Wait a minute,' he said. 'Can your child see?'

30　*'Yes,' she said. 'But I can't.'*

The young man turned. He put one finger on the plate-glass window, pointing.

'Look, Sonny, what's in there?' he asked.

'Not Sonny,' the child objected.

'Go on, Mary. Tell the gentleman,' her mother encouraged her.

35　*'Pretty ladies,' said the child.*

The man took the woman by the arm, and felt his way to the next window.

'And what's in here?' he asked again.

'Apples and fings,' the child told him.

40　*'Fine!' said the young man.*

He pulled off his shoe, and hit the window with a smart smack with the heel of it. He was inexperienced: the first blow did not do it, but the second did. The crash reverberated up and down the street. He restored his shoe, put an arm cautiously through the broken window, and felt about until he found a couple of oranges. One he gave to the woman and one to the child. He felt

45　*about again, found one for himself, and began to peel it. The woman fingered hers.*

'But – ' she began.

'What's the matter? Don't like oranges?' he asked.

'This isn't right,' she said. 'We didn't ought to take 'em. Not like this.'

'How else are you going to get food?' he inquired.

(From *The Day of the Triffids* by John Wyndham, 1951)

1. What atmosphere is created in the first paragraph? (3)

2. How does the writer stress the horror of sudden blindness? (4)

3. What qualities does the author give to the man with the white stick? (6)

4. What effect is created by the introduction of the woman with the child? (6)

5. How does the writer use dialogue and other techniques to shape our response to the horror of the situation? (6)

2. Travel writing

Level 1

Frances Mayes, an American university teacher, and her husband Ed, have bought a house in Tuscany in Italy but it is not yet as they would like it to be.

1   *I admire the beauty of scorpions. They look like black-ink hieroglyphs of themselves. I'm fascinated, too, that they can navigate by the stars, though how they ever glimpse constellations from their usual homes in dusty corners of vacant houses, I don't know. One scurries around in the bidet every morning. Several get sucked into the new vacuum cleaner by mistake, though usually they*

5   *are luckier: I trap them in a jar and take them outside. I suspect every cup and shoe. When I fluff a bed pillow, an albino one lands on my bare shoulder. [...] Other than these inhabitants, the inheritance from the former occupants consists of dusty wine bottles – thousands and thousands in the shed and in the stalls. We fill local recycling bins over and over, waterfalls of glass raining from the boxes we've loaded and reloaded. (Outhouses) are piled with rusted pans, newspapers*

10   *from 1958, wire, paint cans, debris. Whole eco-systems of spiders and scorpions are destroyed, though hours later they seem to have regenerated. I look for old photos or antique spoons but see nothing of interest except some handmade iron tools. [...] One cunningly made tool, an elegant little sculpture, is a hand-sized crescent with a worn chestnut handle. Any Tuscan would recognize it in a second: a tool for trimming grapes.*

15   *When we first saw the house, it was filled with fanciful iron beds with painted medallions of Mary and shepherds holding lambs, wormy chests of drawers with marble tops, cribs, foxed mirrors, cradles, boxes, and lugubrious bleeding-heart religious pictures of the Crucifixion. The owner removed everything [...] except a thirties kitchen cupboard and an ugly red bed that we cannot figure out how to get down the narrow back stairs from the third floor. Finally we take the bed*

20   *apart and throw it piece by piece from the window.*

   Local people, out for afternoon strolls, pause in the road and look up at all the mad activity, the car trunk full of bottles, mattress flying, me screaming as a scorpion falls down my shirt when I sweep the stone walls of the stall, Ed wielding a grim-reaper scythe through the weeds. Sometimes they stop and call up 'How much did you pay for the house?'

25   *I'm taken aback and charmed by the bluntness. 'Probably too much,' I answer. One person remembered that long ago an artist from Naples lived there; for most it has stood empty as far back as they can remember.*

Every day we haul and scrub. We are becoming as parched as the hills around us. We have bought

cleaning supplies, a new stove and fridge. With sawhorses and two planks we set up a kitchen

30 *counter. Although we must bring hot water from the bathroom in a plastic laundry pan, we have a*

surprisingly manageable kitchen. As one who has used Williams-Sonoma as a toy store for years,

I begin to get an elementary sense of the kitchen. Three wooden spoons, two for the salad, one for

stirring. A sauté pan, bread knife, cutting knife, cheese grater, pasta pot, baking dish and stove-top

espresso pot. We brought over some old picnic silverware and bought a few glasses and plates.

35 *Those first pastas are divine. After long work, we eat everything in sight then tumble like field*

hands into bed.

(Abridged from *Under the Tuscan Sun* by Frances Mayes, 1996)

Williams-Sonoma – shops in America selling elaborate kitchenware.

1. Look carefully at paragraph 1.
   What does the writer like about:

   (a) scorpions? (2)

   (b) the tools she finds? (2)

2. Choose two words or phrases from paragraph 1 which show how the writer feels
   about nature. (2)
   Explain your choices. (4)

3. Why do you think the writer tells us what local people have said? (4)

4. Write two quotations which say something vivid or interesting about the house, its
   contents or surroundings. (2)
   Explain what your quotations suggest about the place the writer is describing. (4)

5. The writer and her husband are changing as they work on the house. How do you
   know this? (5)

Level 2

Frances Mayes, an American university teacher, and her husband Ed, have bought a house in
Tuscany in Italy but it is not yet as they would like it to be.

1 *I admire the beauty of scorpions. They look like black-ink hieroglyphs of themselves. I'm fascinated,*

too, that they can navigate by the stars, though how they ever glimpse constellations from their

usual homes in dusty corners of vacant houses, I don't know. One scurries around in the bidet

every morning. Several get sucked into the new vacuum cleaner by mistake, though usually they

5 *are luckier: I trap them in a jar and take them outside. I suspect every cup and shoe. When I fluff*

a bed pillow, an albino one lands on my bare shoulder. We upset armies of spiders as we empty

the closet under the stairs of its bottle collection. Impressive, the long threads for legs and the

fly-sized bodies; I can even see their eyes. Other than these inhabitants, the inheritance from the

former occupants consists of dusty wine bottles – thousands and thousands in the shed and in

10 *the stalls. We fill local recycling bins over and over, waterfalls of glass raining from the boxes we've*

loaded and reloaded. The stalls and limonaia (a garage-sized room on the side of the house once used for storing lemons during the winter) are piled with rusted pans, newspapers from 1958, wire, paint cans, debris. Whole eco-systems of spiders and scorpions are destroyed, though hours later they seem to have regenerated. I look for old photos or antique spoons but see nothing of
15 *interest except some handmade iron tools and a 'priest', a swan-shaped wooden form with a hook for a hanging pan of hot coals, which was pushed under bedcovers in winter to warm the clammy sheets. One cunningly made tool, an elegant little sculpture, is a hand-sized crescent with a worn chestnut handle. Any Tuscan would recognize it in a second: a tool for trimming grapes.*

When we first saw the house, it was filled with fanciful iron beds with painted medallions of Mary
20 *and shepherds holding lambs, wormy chests of drawers with marble tops, cribs, foxed mirrors, cradles, boxes, and lugubrious bleeding-heart religious pictures of the Crucifixion. The owner removed everything – down to the switchplate covers and lightbulbs – except a thirties kitchen cupboard and an ugly red bed that we cannot figure out how to get down the narrow back stairs from the third floor. Finally we take the bed apart and throw it piece by piece from the window.*

25 *The Cortonese, out for afternoon strolls, pause in the road and look up at all the mad activity, the car trunk full of bottles, mattress flying, me screaming as a scorpion falls down my shirt when I sweep the stone walls of the stall, Ed wielding a grim-reaper scythe through the weeds. Sometimes they stop and call up 'How much did you pay for the house?'*

I'm taken aback and charmed by the bluntness. 'Probably too much,' I answer. One person
30 *remembered that long ago an artist from Naples lived there; for most it has stood empty as far back as they can remember.*

Every day we haul and scrub. We are becoming as parched as the hills around us. We have bought cleaning supplies, a new stove and fridge. With sawhorses and two planks we set up a kitchen counter. Although we must bring hot water from the bathroom in a plastic laundry pan, we have a
35 *surprisingly manageable kitchen. As one who has used Williams-Sonoma as a toy store for years, I begin to get an elementary sense of the kitchen. Three wooden spoons, two for the salad, one for stirring. A sauté pan, bread knife, cutting knife, cheese grater, pasta pot, baking dish and stove-top espresso pot. We brought over some old picnic silverware and bought a few glasses and plates. Those first pastas are divine. After long work, we eat everything in sight then tumble like field*
40 *hands into bed.*

(From *Under the Tuscan Sun* by Frances Mayes, 1996)

Williams-Sonoma – shops in America selling elaborate kitchenware.

1.	What does the writer find fascinating about scorpions?	(2)
2.	What interests her about the tools she finds?	(2)
3.	What do you learn about the writer's attitude to nature from the first paragraph?	(4)
4.	What effect is created by the conversations with local people?	(4)
5.	How is contrast used in this passage to create a sense of place?	(6)
6.	How does the writer suggest, in the last paragraph, that as they work on the house, she and Ed are changing?	(7)

3. Biography/Autobiography

Level 1

Actress Meera Syal grew up in the West Midlands, the daughter of parents who had come to England from India in the 1970s to make a better life for themselves and their children.

1   *My mother knew from experience that she would get fewer stares and whispers if she had donned any of the sensible teacher's trouser suits she would wear for school, but for her, looking glamorous in saris and formal Indian suits was part of the English people's education. It was her duty to show them that we could wear discreet gold jewellery, dress in tasteful silks and speak*
5   *English without an accent.*

During our very special shopping outings to Birmingham, she would often pass other Indian women in the street and they would stare at each other in that innocent, direct way of two rare species who have just found out they are vaguely related. These other Indian women would inevitably be dressed in embroidered shalwar kameez suits screaming with green and pinks and
10   *yellows (incongruous with thick woolly socks squeezed into open-toed sandals and men's cardies over their vibrating thin silks, evil necessities in this damn cold country) with bright make-up and showy gold-plated jewellery which made them look like ambulating Christmas trees.*

Mama would acknowledge them with a respectful nod and then turn away and shake her head. 'In the village, they would look beautiful. But not here. There is no sun to light them up. Under
15   *clouds, they look like they are dressed for a discotheque.'*

But she was quiet now, no light in her face. Papa said, 'Have something to eat. A cake. Have one of those … what you like … those meringue things.'

'She won't,' I chipped in, scraping my fork into the spongy belly of my rum baba. 'You know what she will say, I can make this cheaper at home.' […]

20   *'That's enough!' barked Papa. 'Mind your manners now or we're going home!'*

My mother shook her head at him and put her hand over mine. I snatched it away and finished my cake in silence.

My father showed he was sorry by buying me a hot dog on the way home. I sat in the back of the Mini and concentrated on licking the tomato sauce off my fingertips whilst singing 'Bobbing Along
25   *on the Bottom of the Beautiful Briny Sea' in between slurps.*

Mummy and Papa were talking again, soft whispers, sss sss sss, my mother's bracelets jingled as she seemed to wipe something from her face. This was my birthday and they were leaving me out again. I squeezed my hot dog and suddenly the sausage shot into my mouth and lodged into my windpipe. I was too shocked to move, my fingers curled uselessly into my fists. They were still
30   *talking, engrossed, I could see Papa's eyes in the mirror, darting from my mother's face to the unfolding road. I thought of writing SAUSAGE STUCK on the windscreen and then realised I could not spell sausage. I was going to die in the back of the car and somewhere inside me, I felt thrilled. It was so dramatic. This was by far the most exciting thing that had ever happened to me.*

(Abridged from *Anita and Me* by Meera Syal, 1996)

1. Look at paragraph 1.
   How does the writer's mother like to dress? (2)
   Why does she dress in this way? (2)

2. Look at paragraph 1. Sum up how well (or not) the writer gets on with her mother. (4)

3. From the whole passage how well (or not) do the writer's parents get on with each other? (5)

4. Look at the final paragraph. What do you find amusing here?
   You might choose to write about: the stuck sausage, the parents' not noticing, the way the writer exaggerates. (6)

5. What do you learn about the writer from this passage?
   You could include her attitude to her parents, her love of food, her use of language. (6)

Level 2

Actress Meera Syal grew up in the West Midlands, the daughter of parents who had come to England from India in the 1970s to make a better life for themselves and their children.

1   *My mother knew from experience that she would get fewer stares and whispers if she had donned any of the sensible teacher's trouser suits she would wear for school, but for her, looking glamorous in saris and formal Indian suits was part of the English people's education. It was her duty to show them that we could wear discreet gold jewellery, dress in tasteful silks and speak*
5   *English without an accent.*

During our very special shopping outings to Birmingham, she would often pass other Indian women in the street and they would stare at each other in that innocent, direct way of two rare species who have just found out they are vaguely related. These other Indian women would inevitably be dressed in embroidered shalwar kameez suits screaming with green and pinks and
10 *yellows (incongruous with thick woolly socks squeezed into open-toed sandals and men's cardies over their vibrating thin silks, evil necessities in this damn cold country) with bright make-up and showy gold-plated jewellery which made them look like ambulating Christmas trees.*

Mama would acknowledge them with a respectful nod and then turn away and shake her head. 'In the village, they would look beautiful. But not here. There is no sun to light them up. Under clouds,
15 *they look like they are dressed for a discotheque.'*

But she was quiet now, no light in her face. Papa said, 'Have something to eat. A cake. Have one of those … what you like … those meringue things.'

'She won't,' I chipped in, scraping my fork into the spongy belly of my rum baba. 'You know what she will say, I can make this cheaper at home.' My mother never ate out, never, always affronted
20 *by paying for some over-boiled, under-seasoned dish of slop when she knew she could rustle up a hot, heartwarming meal from a few leftover vegetables and a handful of spices. 'I bet you couldn't make this at home,' I continued. 'How would you make a cake? How would you get it round and*

get the cream to stand up and the cherry to balance like this? You have to buy some things, you can't do everything you know …?'

25 'That's enough!' barked Papa. 'Mind your manners now or we're going home!'

My mother shook her head at him and put her hand over mine. I snatched it away and finished my cake in silence.

My father showed he was sorry by buying me a hot dog on the way home. I sat in the back of the Mini and concentrated on licking the tomato sauce off my fingertips whilst singing 'Bobbing Along
30 on the Bottom of the Beautiful Briny Sea' in between slurps.

Mummy and Papa were talking again, soft whispers, sss sss sss, my mother's bracelets jingled as she seemed to wipe something from her face. This was my birthday and they were leaving me out again. I squeezed my hot dog and suddenly the sausage shot into my mouth and lodged into my windpipe. I was too shocked to move, my fingers curled uselessly into my fists. They were still
35 talking, engrossed, I could see Papa's eyes in the mirror, darting from my mother's face to the unfolding road. I thought of writing SAUSAGE STUCK on the windscreen and then realised I could not spell sausage. I was going to die in the back of the car and somewhere inside me, I felt thrilled. It was so dramatic. This was by far the most exciting thing that had ever happened to me.

(From *Anita and Me* by Meera Syal, 1996)

1. What does paragraph 1 tell us:

   (a) about the writer's mother and her attitudes? (2)

   (b) the writer's own feelings about her mother's views? (2)

2. How does the writer indicate the tension between her mother and herself in paragraph 5? (4)

3. What does this passage reveal about the relationship between her parents as observed and remembered by the writer? (5)

4. How does the writer make the final paragraph funny? (6)

5. What impression is the writer trying to create of herself in this passage? (6)

4. Drama

Joey and Topthorn are farm horses. They are being trained to work in the war zones of France in the First World War. In the play the horses are represented by very impressive life-size puppets, each operated by three, visible, puppeteers.

Military Stables, 6 November 1914

Nicholls   (to Joey) *Training's nearly over but you're not ready for war yet.*

Nicholls suddenly fires a round from a pistol near Joey's head. Joey reacts. Nicholls is intending to 'desensitise' Joey – making him used to it.

Good boy. This is a gun. The smell is cordite. Try again.

Fires another round. Joey reacts.

Good boy.

Fires another. Joey reacts.

Good boy, Joey.

Enter Captain Stewart.

Nicholls fires two or three rapid rounds.

Good boy. You'll get used to it … Imagine if these creatures suddenly evolved – that they became as warlike and violent as us.

Stewart   *That's an odd thought.*

Nicholls   *You think I'm odd?*

Stewart   *Oh, no, I didn't mean that, I mean I've never thought that about horses.*

Nicholls   *I hadn't until just then.* (Calls) *Trooper Warren?*

Ned   *Sir!*

Nicholls   (to Stewart) *We're posted to France in the morning.*

Stewart   *In the morning it is.*

Nicholls   *Tell the men to stop polishing.*

Ned   *What, zur?!*

Nicholls   *Battle orders; no polishing – buttons, cap badges, buckles, stirrup irons – let them all go dull. We don't want anything to flash in the sun and give us away – I know, Warren, after all that hard work.*

Ned   *Sir.*

Exit Ned

Nicholls *How's your troop?*

Stewart *Ready for battle, sir.*

Nicholls *I was pleased with the practice charge today. Were you and Topthorn far behind?*

Stewart *We were breathing right down your neck, as you well know. I wouldn't like to be on the wrong end of our charge. My uncle says men tend to go to pieces when our cavalry bear down on them. He's seen men flee or press themselves into the ground. And even if they keep their positions, there weren't many who could face our cavalry and keep their composure – to aim straight as it were. We're going to cut a swathe through Fritz, he won't know what's hit him. He'll wish that he'd never been born, he'll –*

Nicholls *Well, we're about to discover if all that's true, aren't we? I'm not casting aspersions on your uncle's experience, but every generation has to discover things for themselves, don't they? There's some things that can be understood through telling, but other things have to be experienced before they can be fully apprehended. War is one such thing. How do Joey and Topthorn get on?*

Stewart *They're a bit snippy, sir.*

Nicholls *I wasn't imagining it, then. What's that about?*

Stewart *Two proud animals, sir.*

Nicholls *Is Topthorn out in the paddock?*

Stewart *Yes.*

Nicholls *I'll take Joey out to him. Tell the men to prepare, will you? Reveille at five thirty.*

Exit Stewart

The scene becomes a paddock.

Enter Topthorn. Joey and Topthorn react to one another.

> *Joey, listen. Sort out who's in charge. No fighting – save all that for Fritz … You'll be all right, won't you boys? I just hope that I'm up to it when the time comes. You think I'll be up to it?*

Joey and Topthorn are only interested in each other.

Exit Nicholls.

(From *War Horse*, play by Nick Stafford, 2007, based on the novel by Michael Morpurgo, 1982)

Fritz – British slang for a German.
Reveille – army term for morning wake-up call blown on a bugle.

1. Look carefully at the first part of this scene. Why is Nicholls firing bullets near Joey? How is Joey reacting? (1 + 1)

2. Why does Nicholls tell Ned to stop polishing equipment? How do you think Ned reacts and why do you think he reacts in this way? (1 + 2)

3. Choose two words or phrases (from the spoken text or the stage directions) which tell you something interesting about Joey or Topthorn or both. Explain your choices. (2 + 2)

4. Read carefully what Stewart says about fighting. Sum up how he feels about going into battle. (3)

5. There are three men in this scene. Write a sentence or two about each of them, stressing how different they are from each other. (6)

6. Write two quotations which show how tense everyone is in this scene. Explain your choices fully. (2 + 5)

Level 2

Read the extract from *War Horse* above and answer the questions below.

1. Explain why Nicholls is firing bullets near Joey and how you think this could be done on stage. (1 + 2)

2. Why does Nicholls instruct Ned to stop polishing equipment? How do you think Ned reacts and what do you think his reaction suggests? (1 + 2)

3. What do we learn from this extract about the relationship between Joey and Topthorn? (4)

4. What do you deduce from what Stewart says about how he feels about going into battle? (4)

5. How does the playwright suggest the differences between the three men in this scene? (5)

6. If you were directing this scene what instructions would you give to the actors about how to convey tension? Make sure you refer to the text in your answer. (6)

2.5 Summary

You should now know:

- that there are four different types of literary prose comprehension passage which you might be set in Paper 1: fiction, travel writing, (auto)biography and drama
- how to approach the literary comprehension passage in Paper 1
- the style of answer you should use to respond to the questions.

Chapter 3: Poetry comprehension

In Paper 2 Section A you will be given a poem or part of a poem to read. You will then be asked to answer questions or to write about the poem to show how well you have understood and responded to it.

The same poem or extract will be set at both levels. As with the literary prose comprehension the questions and tasks will be set out in more detail at Level 1.

The poetry question is your chance to show that you:

- are aware of how language is used in poetry
- can write what you think based on your reading of the poem
- understand how poets show the reader what they are feeling
- have learnt about metaphor, simile, personification, symbols, irony, alliteration, assonance, rhyme, rhythm and metre and how they can be used.

You should answer the questions using full sentences, unless indicated otherwise.

If you really don't know the answer, make a sensible guess by looking for clues in the poem, and give your reasons.

Spend time thinking and making notes before writing your answers.

If you are asked to use your imagination to continue the theme of a poem, remember that this is still a question to see if you have understood the poem. So the more you base your imaginative answer on what is in the poem, the more marks you will get.

3.1 Poetic techniques

Before you can tackle a poetry comprehension you need an understanding of the techniques poets use to achieve their effects. Think of these as a poet's 'tools' if it helps. The examiners expect you to be familiar with ten key techniques.

> **TOP TIP**
> Remember that good prose writing will use these techniques too.

Metaphor

A metaphor is the comparison of one thing with another by pretending that the thing described really is what it is being compared with.

Metaphors are not literally true. Like personification or a simile (see below) a metaphor is a form of image. The adjective 'metaphorical' and the adverb 'metaphorically' are useful too.

> **Examples:**
>
> *The wind was a torrent of darkness*
>
> *When the road is a ribbon of moonlight*
>
> (Both from 'The Highwayman' by Alfred Noyes)

Simile

A simile is a comparison of one thing with another which makes it clear that it is a comparison by using the word 'like' or 'as'. It is another sort of image.

> **Examples:**
>
> *the Land / Was sodden as the bed of an ancient lake*
>
> *Rain plastered the land till it was shining / Like hammered lead*
>
> (Both from 'November' by Ted Hughes)

Personification

Personification is the giving of human qualities and abilities to non-humans. Poets often personify things as a way of describing them. Personification creates an image or picture in the reader's mind.

> **Examples:**
>
> *The winds were lovesick with her*
>
> (From *Antony and Cleopatra* by William Shakespeare)
>
> *the moon walked the night*
>
> (From 'Silver' by Walter de la Mare)

Symbol

A symbol is an object which stands for something else, as a badge or emblem does. A national flag is a symbol of a country.

> **Examples:**
>
> In 'The Rime of the Ancient Mariner' by Samuel Taylor Coleridge the narrator shoots an albatross and has to wear it round his neck as a punishment. The wearing of the albatross is a symbol of sin.
>
> *A rose by any other name would smell as sweet*
>
> (From *Romeo and Juliet* by William Shakespeare)
>
> The rose is a symbol of Juliet's passionate love for Romeo.
>
> *The merry bells ring*
> *To welcome the spring*
>
> (From 'The Echoing Green' by William Blake)
>
> The bells are a symbol of the change which comes with spring.

Irony

Irony is a figure of speech in which what is said is the opposite of what is meant. It is often 'dry' and funny.

> **Example:**
>
> *Within the human world I know*
> *Such goings on could not be so,*
> *For human beings only do*
> *What their religion tells them to.*
>
> (From 'Diary of a Church Mouse' by John Betjeman)
>
> The poet really means that most people are hypocrites who do exactly the opposite of what their religion tells them to.

Alliteration

Alliteration is the repetition of a consonant sound at the beginning (or sometimes in the middle) of words that are close to each other. You can also use the adjective 'alliterative'.

> **Examples:**
>
> *downward smoke, the slender stream*
>
> (From 'The Lotus-Eaters' by Alfred Lord Tennyson)
>
> *And through his britches the blue winds blow*
>
> (From 'Timothy Winters' by Charles Causley)

Assonance

Assonance is the repetition of the same vowel sound (not necessarily spelt the same way) inside neighbouring words. You can also use the adjective 'assonant'.

> **Examples:**
>
> *plump, unpecked cherries*
>
> (From 'Goblin Market' by Christina Rossetti)
>
> *I've lice in my tunic and a cold in my nose*
>
> (From 'Roman Wall Blues' by W H Auden)

Rhyme

Rhyme is the patterns made by the ends of words which sound the same or similar. There are several sorts of rhyme.

Examples:

> *The Miller was a chap of sixteen stone.*
> *A great stout fellow big in brawn and bone*
>
> > (From *The Canterbury Tales* by Geoffrey Chaucer, translated by Nevil Coghill)

These lines have a full rhyme.

> *My last dear fuel of life to heap upon my soul*
> *And kindle my will to a flame that shall consume*
> *Their dross of indifference and take the toll*
>
> > (From 'Last Lesson of the Afternoon' by D. H. Lawrence)

The first and third lines have a half rhyme – 'soul' and 'toll' almost, but don't quite, rhyme.

> *Where the wheat is sweet as an angel's feet*
>
> > (From 'Cowboy Song' by Charles Causley)

This line has an internal rhyme. The rhyming words are within rather than at the end of the line.

Rhythm

Rhythm is the musical pattern of beats, stressed sounds, unstressed sounds and pauses which give a poem its shape. It can be regular or free.

Examples:

> *Four o'clock strikes,*
> *There's a rising hum,*
> *Then the doors fly open.*
> *The children come*
>
> > (From 'Out of School' by Hal Summers)

The lines above have a regular rhythm with two strong beats in each line (beats underlined).

> *Glory be to God for dappled things*
> *For skies of couple-colour as a brinded cow*
>
> > (From 'Pied Beauty' by Gerard Manley Hopkins)

The lines have a much more regular rhythm, with every second syllable having a stress/beat.

> *Nobody heard him, the dead man,*
> *But still he lay moaning*
> *I was much further out than you thought*
>
> > (From 'Not Waving but Drowning' by Stevie Smith)

The lines above have an irregular rhythm (once again the beats have been underlined).

Metre

Metre is the pattern of sound units in lines of verse. Just as music has bars, separated by bar lines, with up beats and down beats inside them, so lines of poetry are divided into feet like this:

> If <u>mu</u> / sic <u>be</u> / the <u>food</u> / of <u>love</u> / play <u>on</u>
>
> (From *Twelfth Night* by William Shakespeare)
>
> <u>Merri</u>ly / <u>merri</u>ly / <u>shall</u> I live / <u>now</u>
>
> (From *The Tempest* by William Shakespeare)
>
> <u>Bubb</u>le / <u>bubb</u>le / <u>toil</u> and / <u>troub</u>le
>
> (From *Macbeth* by William Shakespeare)

If you say these lines aloud in an exaggerated way you will hear that the rhythm in each of the three lines above is different because of where you have to put the stresses in the feet. For example we say BU-bble not bu-BBLE and MER-ri-ly not mer-ri-LY or mer-RI-ly and this placement of the stress affects the rhythm of our speech.

Using these terms in your writing

Although you need to be familiar with the ten terms above, be careful how you use them. Examiners will not give marks for what they call 'device spotting'. They expect you to use the terms to show how the poet is creating his or her effects.

Imagine you are writing about these opening lines from G K Chesterton's 'The Donkey':

> When fishes flew and forests walked
> And figs grew upon thorn

TOP TIP

Use words such as 'effect' and expressions such as 'The poet asks/wonders/ creates/suggests' in your writing about poetry.

You will get no marks for writing the following and then moving on to another point:

> The poet uses alliteration in the first two lines.

You will, however, get marks for writing something like this:

> The poet's use of alliteration in the first two lines helps to suggest a topsy-turvy ancient world in which nothing is as we know it now. The repeated 'f', a soft sound, makes it sound gentle, reassuring and convincing so that we are drawn into the story – a bit like 'Once upon a time' in a fairy story.

TOP TIP

Do not stop at identifying the poet's tools. Comment on the effects that he or she has created.

Here's another example based on the opening of John Keats's poem 'To Autumn'.

> *Season of mists and mellow fruitfulness,*
> *Close bosom-friend of the maturing sun*

Do not just write:

> *The second line is an example of personification.*

Instead write something such as:

> *The poet personifies the declining sun to suggest that it is a relative of the season autumn (also personified because that's who the poem is addressed to). Together the two are responsible for the ripening of the autumn fruits and the mists as the season changes. By addressing first autumn and then the sun as if they were people Keats creates a sense that the onset of autumn is an intimate, 'hands on' process managed by forces with personalities.*

TOP TIP

It is sometimes easier to comment on a poet's effects if you use adjectives such as 'assonant' or 'ironic' rather than the nouns 'assonance' and 'irony'. Verbs such as 'symbolises' or 'personifies' are useful too.

3.2 Approaching a poem

In your exam you will, almost certainly, be faced with a poem you have never seen before. The examiners want to see how well you can read, understand and respond to it in a fairly short time.

Make sure you spend enough time reading and thinking about the poem before you try to answer the questions.

Read it through quickly once. Then read it a second time more slowly – aloud to yourself in your head – so that you hear the rhyme, rhythm and metre as well as seeing it on the page. Poetry is very close to music. It needs to be heard as well as read if you're going to respond to it fully. Listen inside your head to the sound of the poem's words while you are in your exam.

When you are reading look closely at the poem's punctuation to make sure you get the full sense of its meaning.

Remember that:

- sentences and phrases do not always finish at the ends of lines
- full stops, commas and other marks of punctuation are often placed in the middle of lines
- sometimes there is no punctuation at the ends of stanzas because sentences flow from one stanza to the next.

Read the poem a third time. Then tackle the questions.

3.3 Sample questions and answers

Try these yourself, covering up the sample answer. Then, when you've written your own response, compare it with the one given here.

Remember, though, that there are very few absolutely right or absolutely wrong answers in English. The important thing is for you to be able to back up your answer with evidence from the poem.

The suggestions given here are merely one possible response. There will be others.

Sample 1

> *My father worked with a horse-plough,*
> *His shoulders globed like a full sail strung*
> *Between the shafts and the furrow.*
> *The horses strained at his clicking tongue*

(From 'Follower' by Seamus Heaney)

Level 1 question

How can you tell that the poet's father is strong and hard working from this stanza? (3 marks)

Answer

His father has big rounded shoulders ('globed') like a billowing sail as he controls his plough horses. He and the horses are a powerful team and the animals respond by pulling harder ('strained') when they hear his 'clicking tongue'. The rhyming of 'strung' and 'tongue' helps to suggest the rhythm of the continuous efforts of the man and his horses.

Level 2 question

What impressions of the poet's father are created in this stanza? (4 marks)

Answer

His father is presented as very strong, his shoulders are rounded ('globed') like a billowing sail as he controls his plough horses. He and the horses are a team and they respond by pulling harder ('strained') at the sound of his 'clicking tongue'. The rhyming of 'strung' and 'tongue' and half-rhyming 'plough' and 'furrow' help to reinforce the rhythm of the work of the man and his horses. Although the work is simple and earthy, there is also an elegance and precision to it. The sails in the poet's simile are delicate, which makes for an interesting contrast.

TOP TIP
Read some unfamiliar poems (any anthology will provide some) and think about how you would respond to them in an exam.

Sample 2

I was angry with my friend
I told my wrath, my wrath did end
I was angry with my foe
I told it not, my wrath did grow.

(From 'A Poison Tree' by William Blake)

Level 1 question

How do you know, from this stanza, that the poet thinks it is better to talk about anger than to say nothing? (2 marks)

Answer

This stanza is in two halves and it reminds me of a nursery rhyme or proverb which is supposed to teach you something. The first half says that when he talked about his anger to a friend – 'told my wrath' – it went away. But the second half says that when he 'told it not' – to an enemy – it stayed and got worse. The language is very simple as if it's written for children.

Level 2 question

How does the poet communicate his point in this stanza? (3 marks)

Answer

This stanza is like a nursery rhyme or a proverb. It uses very simple language – almost all the words have just one syllable so it's quite childlike – and no imagery or anything sophisticated to say that when he 'told his wrath', or talked about his anger, it disappeared. On the other hand, the second half of the perfectly balanced stanza with its firm rhyming pairs of lines, says that bottled-up anger ('I told it not') will grow, and by implication turn into something more serious. It is significant too that in the first two lines he is thinking about being angry with a friend and in the second two an enemy.

Sample 3

I leant upon a coppice gate
When Frost was spectre-gray
And Winter's dregs made desolate
The weakening eye of day

(From 'The Darkling Thrush' by Thomas Hardy)

Level 1 question

How can you tell from this stanza that it is late on a winter afternoon? (3 marks)

Answer

It must be cold because the 'spectre-gray' frost is creating a ghostly atmosphere. The metaphorical 'dregs' of winter suggest that this is towards the end of winter — like the last drop in the bottom of a cup or glass. The personification of day with its 'weakening eye' shows that the light is fading.

Level 2 question

What atmosphere is created in this stanza? (3 marks)

Answer

It is a late winter's afternoon and it is very cold. The poet is in a rural place, perhaps on the edge of a wood ('coppice gate') and the 'spectre-gray' frost is creating a ghostly atmosphere in the fading light. The metaphorical 'dregs' of winter suggest that this is towards the end of winter — like the last drop in the bottom of a cup or glass. The personification of day with its 'weakening eye' adds to the sense of gloom and creates a rather despondent mood.

Sample 4

I'll never be a lap dog licking dirty feet,
A sleek dog, a meek dog, cringing for my meat,
Not for me the fireside or the well-filled plate,
But shut door, and sharp stone, and cuff and kick, and hate.

(From 'Lone Dog' by Irene McLeod)

Level 1 question

How can you tell, from this stanza, that the dog narrating the poem is fierce? (2 marks)

Answer

He despises dogs which are 'sleek' or 'meek' and dependent on human beings for a 'well-filled plate'. The repetition of 'and' four times in the fourth line sounds as if the dog is barking out his aggression. The final line, with strong aggressive words, indicates his fierceness.

Level 2 question

How does the poet convey the dog's personality in this stanza? (4 marks)

Answer

The alliterative first line ('lap', 'licking', 'dog', 'dirty') and the internal rhyme of 'sleek' and 'meek' in the second combine with the regular metre and tight end rhymes to make the lines move energetically like a dog running or panting. The use of the negatives 'never' and 'not' introduce a note of pride into the narrative voice. He despises dogs which are 'sleek' or 'meek' and dependent on human beings for a 'well-filled plate'. The repetition of 'and' four times in the fourth line sounds very determined and definite as if the dog is barking out his aggression.

> **TOP TIP**
> Choose a short poem from an anthology. Read it carefully. Then write your own six questions based on it. If you do this with a partner you could then swap poems and answer each other's questions as a revision exercise.

3.4 Practice task

Now try this exercise which is similar to a Paper 2 Section A task.

The marks at the end of each question are a guide as to how much you should write in your answers.

You should spend around 35 minutes on the task. Spend the first 5 minutes planning. Write for about 25 minutes. Read your work through in the last 5 minutes to check for mistakes and to make small changes.

There are suggestions to show you how to write good answers in Chapter 6. Do not look at these until you've tried this task yourself. Then consult the suggestions to see how you might have done it better.

Sunken Evening

1   *The green light floods the city square —*
A sea of fowl and feathered fish,
Where squalls of rainbirds dive and splash
And gusty sparrows chop the air.

5   *Submerged, the prawn-blue pigeons feed*
In sandy grottoes round the Mall,
And crusted lobster-buses crawl
Among the fountains' silver weed.

    There, like a wreck, with mast and bell,
10 *The torn church settles by the bow,*
While phosphorescent starlings stow
Their mussel shells along the hull.

    The oyster-poet, drowned but dry,
Rolls a black pearl between his bones;
15 *The typist, trapped by telephones,*
Gazes in bubbles at the sky.

    Till, with the dark, the shallows run,
And homeward surges tide and fret —
The slow night trawls its heavy net
20 *And hauls the clerk to Surbiton.*

                   Laurie Lee

Level 1

1.   Look at stanza 3. How can you tell that the starlings are settling down for the night?   (1)

2.   Look at stanza 4.
      Why does the narrator think the typist is trapped?   (2)
      Why is the poet compared with an oyster?   (2)

3.   Write two quotations which show that the poet is comparing the city with an underwater scene.   (2)
      Explain your choices.   (4)

4.   What changes in the last verse and how do you know?   (4)

5.   Write three quotations which show that this poem is set in London.   (2)
      Explain your choices.   (3)

6.   Imagine you are a clerk who lives in Surbiton. Write an account of your journey home using what you have learned from the poem.   (5)

1. Comment on the poet's reference to the starlings in the third stanza. (3)

2. Explain what the poet is comparing the city with. Refer closely to several words from different stanzas in your answer. (4)

3. Re-read the fourth stanza. Why does the poet think the typist is trapped and why is the poet compared with an oyster? Refer closely to the poem to support your ideas. (4)

4. What changes in the last stanza? How does the poet describe this change? (1 + 2)

5. The poet doesn't tell us the exact place that this poem describes. Where do you think it is? Include at least three quotations in your answer. (6)

6. How do you respond to this poem? Support your answer by referring closely to the poem. (5)

3.5 Summary

You should now know:

- how to approach the poetry comprehension questions of the 13+ exam
- the different techniques which poets use and the names for them
- how to use your understanding of these terms in your answers.

Chapter 4: Writing for practical purposes

You will be asked to write two compositions in your 13+ Common Entrance exams. This applies to both Level 1 and Level 2 candidates.

Your first writing task is in Paper 1. It gives you the opportunity to show that you can use language to:

- argue
- persuade
- explain
- advise
- inform.

There is also the option, in Paper 1, to demonstrate these skills by writing about one or more novels or other texts (such as a set of short stories, a play, biography or travel book) which you have studied in class or read for yourself. The examiners will not direct you to write about a specific text. They will, instead, offer you a general writing task which you can apply to any text you have read and choose to write about.

The reading-related task will give you the opportunity to write about:

- dramatic moments
- episodes in which development and change take place
- contrasts between, for example, characters, places or events
- various other ideas in your chosen text such as themes or setting.

The other options in this section will be tasks similar to the following:

- Write a detailed description of a place which you have visited on holiday in a way which either recommends it warmly or makes it clear that it is not, in your opinion, worth going to.

- Write about an occasion when you were worried or in danger. What did you do and why?

- Knowledge and ignorance. Think about the advantages and disadvantage of knowing and not knowing things. Argue the importance of one over the other – with examples. Write about the advantages and disadvantages of each.

You might be asked to write your responses in the form of:

- a letter
- an email
- a magazine or newspaper article
- a speech
- a format which it is left to you to choose – usually simply a composition.

Exercise

For practice, choose one of the ideas above – or invent a similar one of your own – and practise with it. Make sure you spend at least 5 minutes planning it and making notes. Allow yourself about 30 minutes' writing time.

4.1 Writing from personal experience

Writing an account of something which has happened to you could include several types of writing. If, for example you are writing about an accident you have experienced you might also be arguing for better safety procedures or explaining your point of view. Or an account of sports day at school might involve advising schools and teachers how to manage such events better or persuading parents not to embarrass their children.

If you opt for this sort of writing:

- make it witty if you can

- remember that smiling at yourself as you look back often works well

- don't be afraid to express yourself in an unusual or original way.

Sample 1

Look at this very short extract, from a personal account of a concert which went wrong, as an example:

> *The good news is that I come in bang on time, on the first beat. The bad news is that everyone else is playing the wrong music in the wrong key. This never used to matter when I played keyboard for the Clun Symphonique de Limoges with whom we once managed to get through an entire concert with the flautist playing one whole piece ahead of the rest of us. And nobody noticed.*
>
> (Michael Wright, the *Daily Telegraph*, 22nd December 2012)

Points to note

The writer:

- uses irony to show that he did not come in at the right time and/or play in tune. He pretends he did and that everyone else in the group was wrong

- makes a joke about an earlier concert which had gone even more disastrously wrong

- is very open about his musical shortcomings

- uses the present tense to give his anecdote immediacy

- varies the length of his sentences.

TOP TIP

When you are planning your exam answer, list the points you want to make. Each point may become a paragraph or may be subdivided into shorter paragraphs.

Exercise

Practise your skills by writing a paragraph of your own about an occasion when something went wrong in your life. Try to be witty and limit yourself to four sentences of varying length as Michael Wright does.

4.2 Writing to argue or persuade

Some writing tasks invite you to write your views on something people disagree about. Often this involves writing persuasively.

For example:

- There has been much debate about what children should and should not eat as a regular part of their diet. What are your own thoughts on this subject?

- Fox hunting has been banned in England. What are your views about this?

- What are your own thoughts on the subject of television?

> *TV rots the senses in the head!*
> *It kills the imagination dead!*
> *It clogs and clutters up the mind!*
> *It makes the child so dull and blind!*
>
> (From *Charlie and the Chocolate Factory* by Roald Dahl, 1964)

Do you agree with this sentiment?

Obviously, if you choose an option such as this you will have a view of your own and the purpose of your writing will be to persuade others to agree with you.

Make your case

Your job is to set down what you think and to explain why you think this as persuasively as you can.

When you are planning your writing, note any evidence you can think of to support your views. Your evidence might, for example, be from your own experience, things you have read or heard of in the media (such as newspapers, television or the internet), information you have been given by your teachers or parents, or anything you have noticed or learnt from other sources.

For example, if you are writing about healthy eating, you might mention children you know who eat unusually healthily or unhealthily, facts and figures (if you know them) about children becoming less healthy and fatter because of the food many of them eat, and differences parents and schools can make, with examples.

Or, if you are arguing that there is nothing wrong with children's diets, then mention some supporting evidence to prove your points. And/or you might decide to mention your views about the responsibility adults have towards children's eating and whether or not most of them set a good example. If so, again, you will need some evidence.

Useful words and phrases for opinion essays and other forms of persuasive writing:

- I contend/believe/think/suggest/propose/insist …

- Take … (at the beginning of a sentence to introduce an example)

- What is more …
- Moreover …
- Nevertheless/nonetheless …
- I would argue …
- Evidence suggests …
- Historically/traditionally …
- In the past …
- Some people think …
- I wonder …

TOP TIP

Newspaper columnists often use the formula of an anecdote followed by evidence. Read as many columns as you can — particularly in the weekend newspapers — as part of your revision.

Start with an anecdote

A piece of writing to persuade or inform often works well if you start with an anecdote (a little story about something which has happened to you or someone you know, or something you saw). You can then widen out your argument with evidence and end with a comment which links the evidence to your anecdote.

For example, in this letter to the *Daily Telegraph* (on 27th January 2013), writer Paul Vincent starts with something he has done himself (donated a piano) before approvingly describing a scheme to make use of unwanted pianos.

> *I have put an otherwise unwanted piano in an empty shop in my local town.*
>
> *The Pianos in Accessible New Outlets project is endorsed by our town council and arts centre and provides a community service to anyone wanting to play. The premises are unmanned and users pick up a key from a local bookshop.*

Examples of writing to persuade or inform

Sample 2

Study this extract from a blog published on *The Independent's* website in November 2012:

> *Every child should spend part of every school day reading silently. Renaissance Reading offers computer-based schemes to encourage that but, although many schools have had some success with these, I find them a bit mechanical and I think you can encourage reading without them.*
>
> *Actually it's easy. All a school has to do is to put books and reading at the centre of what it does. Teachers and other adults in schools should be talking about reading and being seen to read themselves. For at least half an hour a day everyone should read — including the adults. Nothing is more important and example works wonders. Wise teachers let pupils choose their own books and don't worry too much about quality at first. The important thing is to build reading stamina — in a world when there are many distractions.*
>
> (Susan Elkin)

Points to note

The writer:

- uses the first person ('I find' and 'I think') to share her views and make it clear that she is basing what she says on experience
- writes some short sentences for dramatic effect and to make the writing sharp and direct ('Every child should spend part of every day reading silently', 'Actually it's easy')
- is very firm ('Nothing is more important and example works wonders')
- is not afraid to give teachers some strong advice – without being rude ('Teachers and other adults in school should …' and 'Wise teachers ….')
- moves smoothly from one point to the next.

Sample 3

Look closely at this example of opinion writing which uses a different style from the one above.

> *I am partial to the occasional bag of crisps. The brand I buy claims to be 'handmade'. How? They sell tons of the things in shops across the land. Am I really supposed to believe that vast teams of workers spend their lives making crisps by hand? Don't they have <u>any</u> machines in their factories? And how do you 'hand make' a crisp anyway? A piece of pottery or a nice hand-knitted sweater perhaps, but a crisp?*

> (John Humphrys, *Beyond Words*, 2006)

Points to note

The writer:

- begins with a clear statement
- draws attention to the word he is querying – 'handmade' – in the second
- ridicules the use of the word 'handmade' by making statements in the form of questions
- is not afraid to use non-grammatical 'sentences' such as the last one
- makes his writing very comfortable and accessible by using relaxed expressions such as 'tons of the things' and 'nice hand-knitted sweater'
- is upbeat and amusing.

> **TOP TIP**
> Asking questions and making it obvious that you and your reader know the answer to them can be a useful way of arguing a point and persuading your reader to your point of view.

Exercise

For practice, choose one of the ideas at the beginning of this section – or invent a similar one of your own – and practise with it. Make sure you spend at least five minutes planning it and making notes. Allow yourself about 30 minutes' writing time.

4.3 Writing to advise or inform

Some writing tasks invite you to discuss someone else's problem, perhaps in the form of a letter or email. Or, as part of the same question, you could be asked to share information.

For example:

- Explain to a friend in a letter how you have taken up a new hobby, sport or pastime. Tell him or her what the activity involves and give reasons why your friend should join you.

- Write an article for the school magazine, newspaper, newsletter or website to help new students. Tell them what they need to know about the school, from a pupil's point of view, and give any advice which you think newcomers need.

- Imagine that someone you know has emailed you for advice about a problem. Write your answer.

When you are sharing information or advising:

- be as clear and concise as you can

- set your points down step by step, perhaps in short paragraphs

- use accurate terminology if your writing relates to a specific activity.

Example of writing to advise or inform

Sample 4

Dear Granny

I'm so glad you have decided to buy a computer. I'm sure you won't regret it and soon you'll be able to email me – and we can exchange messages on Facebook and Twitter.

You asked my advice about what sort of computer to buy. Well, I think you have four options to choose from.

First, you could buy a big desktop computer like the one in Dad's study. It would take up a fair amount of room, though, because you'd need a screen, keyboard and computer 'box' which are all separate. You'll need to decide whether you have room for this.

Second, you might consider a laptop like mine. It has a reasonable size screen and keyboard but it's all in one so it doesn't take up much room and you can easily carry it around the house although you might find it rather heavy to take out in a bag.

Third, a netbook might suit you – really just a mini laptop. These are really light and portable and you could carry it around very easily. The best ones have a reasonable size keyboard and a small screen.

Fourth, they're more expensive than small laptops but you could think about a tablet – such as an iPad. They are very portable, fine for email and using the Internet for lots of things. They also act as book readers and excellent cameras. But they don't have a proper keyboard. How much typing are you expecting to do?

Points to note

This is, obviously, part of a letter from a grandchild to a grandmother. Notice that the writer:

- thinks the points through carefully and numbers them

- shares information but keeps it very basic, assuming that her grandmother knows very little

- uses technical terms (desktop, laptop, iPad) but keeps these to a minimum

- focuses on practical matters such as the space in her grandmother's home

- uses expressions appropriate to advice such as 'might suit you', 'you could', 'you might'

- mentions things he/she assumes her grandmother will have noticed such as 'the one in Dad's study' as a basic way of explaining to a beginner what a desktop computer is.

> **TOP TIP**
> When you write to inform or advise think carefully about who the writing is for and write appropriately for that person.

Exercise

For practice, choose one of the ideas at beginning of this section – or invent a similar one of your own – and practise with it. Make sure you spend at least 5 minutes planning it and making notes. Allow yourself about 30 minutes' writing time.

4.4 Writing a book-related composition

As we have seen, one of the writing options in Paper 2 invites you to write about books you have read.

You may base your answer on any book or books you have read in or out of school – and it can be a play text as well as any kind of fiction or non-fiction book.

Remember: the question is always a general one which doesn't specify any particular books. This is so that you can answer it with reference to any book you wish.

At the top of your answer always write the title and author of the book(s) you have chosen to write about.

You are likely to be asked to do some of the following:

- write about the impact a book has had on you

- make general points about reading with reference to books you have read

- write about your reading in various other ways.

Express, compare, state

You will always get higher marks if you:

- express your opinions rather than use too much of your space/time simply retelling the story or describing what the book is about

- compare a book with other books or, for example, a main character from one book with characters from other books. For example:

    Tom from Goodnight Mister Tom *is rather like Silas in* Silas Marner. *Each is a lonely old man who comes to life when a child comes to live with him.*

- state your preferences and give reasons for them. For example:

    I admired the characterisation in Noughts and Crosses. *Malorie Blackman's decision to have both Sephy and Callum as alternating narrators means that you keep seeing characters such as their parents from different points of view. It makes for a really rounded account of Callum and Sephy and their misunderstandings too.*

This explains very specifically what the reader liked about the author's way of telling the story. Do not write:

Noughts and Crosses *is a brilliant book with really good characters and I recommend it for people my age.*

This says nothing at all about the book, only that the reader liked it. Actually there is no evidence in this sentence that the writer has even read it.

TOP TIP

Don't be afraid, if it is appropriate, to mention in your exam a book you did **not** enjoy. As long as you give reasons for your views and preference.

In general, it is probably safer to choose texts you have studied in school rather than those you have read individually at home. If you have worked on something as a class text, your teacher will have helped you to learn more about it. You will have taken part in class discussions and you have probably already done some written work connected with the book as part of your class work. You will, therefore, find it easier to write thoughtfully about it in your exam than if you try to write about something you have read casually and quickly on your own.

Stick to the book

When you're writing about a book try to avoid loose phrases and statements which don't refer specifically to what is in the text. For example, the following sentences would not add much to your writing and would not get you many marks:

- This is a wonderful book and I have recommended it to all my friends.
- I give this great book five stars.
- I shall never forget this book.
- I couldn't put this book down.
- It's a great page-turner.
- This is the best book I have ever read.
- My mum and dad both think it is a good book too.
- A great book for all ages

Use the content

Think of the content of the book as evidence. Use it and refer to it to support the points you make.

Useful phrases and statements for book-related compositions:

- X is the best of the three books by Y I have read because …
- B, with its …, … plot and …, … characters, is …
- I enjoyed/admired the episode in which … because …
- The characters are …
- The plot is …
- This play is better than … because …

TOP TIP

Remember that in an exam you are not trying to 'sell' the book or books to the examiner. Rather, you are trying to show him or her how thoughtfully you have read it and how well you can communicate your ideas about it in writing.

Don't be vague

Avoid vague words like 'good', 'great' and 'wonderful'. Instead use specific words such as 'convincing', 'vulnerable' or 'menacing' to describe characters, or 'twisted', 'satisfying', 'puzzling' or 'well constructed' to describe a plot. If it's a non-fiction book use words like 'informative', 'provocative', 'detailed'.

Refer to the author

Refer to the author in your writing as much as you can. Below are some verbs and phrases to help you comment on what the author is doing.

The author (or use his or her surname):

- presents
- wants us to see that
- leads us to think that
- gives us
- offers us
- seems to think
- has a habit of

TOP TIP

Look particularly at how the author uses dialogue. What does it add to the story? What does it tell you about the characters?

Example of a book-related essay

This is an example of the sort of Paper 2 essay which will please examiners. It refers to Michelle Magorian's 1981 novel *Goodnight Mister Tom* which many of you will have read. Look at it closely. Notice how the writer stresses the drama, transition and contrast which he or she finds in the chosen text.

Sample

Question

Write about a book which has impressed you and explain why you admire it.

Answer

Goodnight Mister Tom is a story about the evacuation of children out of London to the safety of the countryside. Although I have read other evacuation stories (*Carrie's War* by Nina Bawden and *Fireweed* by Jill Paton Walsh, for example) this is the one which had the most impact on me.

That is, I think, mostly because of the strength of the characterisation and the way in which Magorian offers us contrasts and similarities between her characters to reflect upon. For example, Tom is, in some ways, like Willie. He is damaged, troubled and lonely – although much kinder than the villagers initially think he is – and it isn't until he meets, and has to be responsible for, the equally damaged Willie, with his background of abuse, that he finds a real purpose in life. The way in which Tom and Willie gradually change and heal each other is deeply moving, especially at the very end when Willie unthinkingly addresses Tom as Dad and Magorian makes it clear that now these two have each other permanently everything will be all right.

There are other contrasts between characters too. Tom is very different from the only other parent figure Willie has known – his mentally ill mother who has severe religious mania, but also works as a prostitute and beats Willie severely as well as locking him in a cupboard with his doomed baby sister. Willie himself, at first very diffident – is also contrasted with the ebullient, theatrical Zach who comes from a middle-class background.

Magorian also makes us strongly aware of the contrast between settings. Willie has come from Deptford, then a poor area in south London. Tom's cottage, the village and the church next door are very rural and there's a strong sense there of pulling together in war. We become aware of just how stark the difference is when Willie's mother summons him home and, worried at not hearing from the boy, Tom goes to London to look for him. The author makes us see the horror of war-torn London from Tom's point of view as he gets caught up in an air raid and, eventually, traces Willie to his mother's home. The third environment is the London hospital where Willie is taken for some pretty horrifying treatment which is forced on him. It too contrasts with both Little Weirwold and the streets of London.

Although there is a story with a happy ending at the heart of this novel, it is neither sentimental nor romantic which is part of its appeal. There is a lot of death in the narrative so it reflects real life – especially in war time. Mrs Hartridge's husband, David, is killed in action. Willie has to come to terms with the tragic death of his always cheerful friend Zach in an air raid and with the death of the baby sister (from neglect) he found back in London as well as his mother's suicide. Magorian also gives us a lovely passage in the churchyard when Tom explains to Willie that his wife, Rachel and their child, died many years before, which explains why he has been so withdrawn and bad-tempered for so long.

Goodnight Mister Tom is a very dramatic story with its quiet interludes, sudden deaths, noisy scenes in London – and the almost constant presence of Tom's faithful, sensitive dog Sammy who is, in effect, another character. This element is part of the reason it is so powerful. It is not surprising that it has been made into both a TV film and a stage play, both of which I've seen but neither has the impact of the book which is so much more detailed.

Points to note

This essay:

- shows a detailed knowledge of *Goodnight Mister Tom*
- provides evidence that the writer has read the book thoughtfully
- compares it with other similar books and with adaptations for stage and screen
- comments on characterisation
- focuses on Magorian's skill in creating interesting contrasts
- tells the examiner how the candidate responds to the book
- is carefully structured with an introduction and conclusion
- demonstrates most of the points made in this chapter about book-related tasks!

Exercise

Write about any book you have read recently. Explain in detail what you thought of it and why.

4.5 Practice tasks

This is an example of the choice you can expect in Paper 1 Section B. Use the tasks for practice.

You should spend around 40 minutes in total on each task. Spend the first 5 minutes planning. Write for about 30 minutes. Read your work through in the last 5 minutes to check for mistakes and to make small changes.

1. A difficult decision.
   Was there a time when you had to make a difficult decision? How did you eventually decide what to do?
   Write about it in the form of an email to a friend.

2. Sport in school should be optional.
   Imagine you are taking part in a debate with this statement as the proposal.
   Write a speech in which you argue either for or against it.

3.   Think about a time when you, or a member of your family, did something you later regretted. Describe it in an entertaining and humorous way.

4.   EITHER

(a) 'Books are uniquely portable magic' (Stephen King)
   Have you ever read a book which for you was 'portable magic'?
   Explain why it impressed you so much.

OR

(b) 'A really good book needs three things: strong characters, a good plot and something to make you think.'
   Explain how far you agree with this statement by referring to your own reading.

Chapter 5: Creative writing

Paper 2 invites you to write in an original, fictional, imaginative way.

This chapter therefore looks at some of the general skills that are required for writing well and then goes on to focus on the skills you need for writing stories and descriptions, including how to create convincing characters and dialogue.

Paper 2 will give you a choice of subjects to write about. The paper usually includes options such as:

- a story
- an imaginative description
- a quotation, statement or title which you can respond to in any imaginative way you wish.

You must choose **one** of these.

The same options for writing are offered at both levels.

> **TOP TIP**
> Remember that you are free to write in any way you wish but your use of language needs to be appropriate and accurate.

The examiner wants you to be as free as possible to show how well you can use language imaginatively, to write descriptively and to tell stories. That is why the suggestions you are given to choose from are quite vague and open ended.

It is important that you:

- write in an appropriate way for the task you have chosen
- spell correctly
- punctuate and use grammar properly
- use exciting vocabulary accurately.

5.1 Writing well

Here are some practical ideas to help you improve the quality of your writing.

> **TOP TIP**
> As you revise, try writing paragraphs with sentences of different lengths. Look out for sentences of different lengths while you're reading too.

Sentence length

Vary the length of your sentences. A piece of writing in which all the sentences are roughly the same length is usually dull and flat.

Look at an example of a professional writer using sentences of different lengths:

> *Her beauty silenced us. Despite Kenji's enthusiasm earlier, I was quite unprepared for it. I thought then that I understood Lady Maruyana's suffering: at least part of it had to be jealousy. How could any man refuse the possession of such beauty?*
>
> (From *Across the Nightingale Floor* by Lian Hearn, 2002)

In one paragraph Lian Hearn has a sequence of sentences which have – in order – 4, 10, 18 and 10 words. Read it aloud. You will notice that varied sentence and word length creates rhythm, which matters as much in prose as in poetry. The stresses in the words rise and fall in an irregular way but the writing sounds complete and elegant because of its prose rhythm.

One technique is to build a paragraph of three sentences, each one shorter than the one before. It is quite dramatic and makes your reader want to hurry on to the next paragraph. Here are two examples of professional writers using this techique:

> *Becky knew her tirade had gone too far, that she'd spoiled the day, that it would make her mother cry, and that she'd hate herself later for making her unhappy again. But to her surprise, her mother didn't cry this time. Instead she went very quiet.*
>
> (From *Best Mate* by Michael Morpurgo, 2007)
>
> *Something stirred in the study window and a glow of light shone out for a moment. She remembered what she had to do and tapped on the glass door. It opened almost at once.*
>
> (From *Northern Lights* by Philip Pullman, 1995)

Sentence shape

Make sure that you vary the shapes of your sentences too. If you are writing a story about Josh don't start the first five sentences with 'Josh' or 'he' followed by a verb.

Instead:

- Start sometimes with a fronted clause or phrase, for example:

  Knowing that he was already late, Josh …
  Desperate and angry, Josh …

- Write an occasional 'inside out' sentence. So, instead of:

  Josh ran as fast as he could because Mia was in terrible danger;

  write:

  Because he knew Mia was in terrible danger, Josh ran as fast as he could.

- If you're writing conversation, vary the position of the words which explain who is speaking. They can go at the beginning, in the middle or at the end of spoken words. Change the order of them too. Use 'Martha said' as well as 'said Martha':

  Freddy said, 'I don't believe a word of it. It just can't be true.'
  'I don't believe a word of it. It just can't be true,' said Freddy.
  'I don't believe a word of it,' said Freddy. 'It just can't be true.'

- Stir some indirect speech into the mix of conversation too:

  Freddy said he didn't believe a word of it because it just couldn't be true.

- Start some sentences with adverbs such as 'hurriedly', 'anxiously', 'now' or 'there', for example:

  There, in the garden, Felicity waited.
  Hurriedly, he leapt on his bike and began to pedal.

- Experiment occasionally with putting the verb before the subject in some of your sentences. For example:

> Suddenly, up jumped the dog.
> Downhill marched the group towards the village.

Study this example of a professional writer varying the shape of her sentences:

> *Uncle Acquila lived on the extreme edge of Calleva. One reached his house down a narrow side street that turned off not far from the East Gate, leaving behind the forum and the temples, and coming to a quiet angle of the old British earthworks – for Calleva had been a British Dun before it became a Roman city – where the hawthorn and hazel still grew and the shyer woodland birds still came. It was much like the other houses of Calleva, timbered and red-roofed and comfortable, built round three sides of a tiny courtyard that was smoothly turfed and set about with imported roses and gum-cistus growing in tall stone jars. But it had one peculiarity: a squat, square, flat-roofed tower rising from one corner: for Uncle Acquila. Having lived most of his life in the shadow of watch-towers from Memphis to Segedunum, he could not be comfortable without one.*
>
> (From *The Eagle of the Ninth* by Rosemary Sutcliff, 1954)

Rosemary Sutcliff uses compound and complex sentences (interspersed with simple ones like the one which opens her paragraph) and often punctuates them with colons and semi-colons.

Note

Colons are used to indicate that another statement is following. Semi-colons are sometimes used in place of commas or full stops for extra strength. (For more on colons and semi-colons, see Chapter 6.)

> **TOP TIP**
>
> As you revise, practise writing paragraphs consisting of sentences of different shapes. Notice and think about sentence shape while you're reading too.

Verbs and nouns, adverbs and adjectives

It is not usually good style to clutter up your writing with too many adjectives and adverbs or descriptive clauses. Instead, choose strong and appropriate verbs and nouns.

Use adverbs and adjectives only if they are really necessary or add something.

In each of the following examples, the first sentence is much better than the second:

1. The water <u>trickled</u> along the <u>gully</u>.
2. A *small* amount of water ran *slowly* along the bottom of the *steep little* valley.

1. <u>Musicologists</u> have found the <u>manuscript</u> of one of Beethoven's <u>overtures</u> in an <u>attic</u> in Vienna.
2. *Music* experts have found Beethoven's *original handwritten* copy of one of his *short* pieces in a *top-floor* room in Vienna.

1. When she heard the fire alarm, Amelia <u>stiffened</u>.
2. When she heard the fire alarm, Amelia felt *nervous and worried*.

1. Goliath *strode* towards David.
2. Goliath walked *determinedly with big steps* towards David.

(Strong, appropriate nouns and verbs are underlined. Avoidable adjectives and adverbs are in italics.)

TOP TIP
Using strong verbs and nouns usually means shorter sentences too – which helps you to vary the shape of your sentences.

Avoid using adjectives and adverbs that add nothing to your writing. They can even weaken the effect of a strong verb or noun.

In the following examples, the first option is stronger and clearer and therefore carries more weight:

1. I am exhausted.
2. I am really exhausted.

1. He apologised.
2. He apologised very sincerely.

If you feel tempted to use the adverb 'actually', or the adjective 'actual', ask yourself if you really need it. Try your sentence without it. You may be surprised how well it works when it is free of these 'clutter' words.

TOP TIP
Make a mental list of adjectives and adverbs which you rarely need. Start it with: very, actually, extremely, awfully …

Repetition

Apart from words such as 'and' and 'the', try to avoid repeating words in your writing.

Look at this example:

> *At moonrise I walked on, not ceasing until I at last reached the foot of the Black Mountains. Here I settled, and chewed upon more of Dahtet's dried meat. Then I lay upon the dusty ground that I might refresh my body with some little sleep. Across the flat land Golahka would come at dawn, and this time I knew he would cross swiftly meaning to reach our camp before I did.*
>
> (From *Apache* by Tanya Landman, 2007)

The writer uses 'cross' to avoid repeating 'walked' or 'walk'. 'Ceasing', 'settled' and 'lay' all have a sense of stopping to rest but there is no repetition.

The better your vocabulary, the easier this is.

If you're writing about people, try not to repeat their names more often than necessary. Of course you can use pronouns such as 'he', 'she' or 'they' but take care that it's clear exactly to whom they refer.

TOP TIP
A good personal word bank comes from reading widely, so make sure you read as many books as you can while you are revising.

For occasional variety use words and phrases to refer to your characters such as:

- the boy/girl/man/woman
- the pupil/child/student
- the teacher/lorry driver/solicitor (or any other profession)
- her/his friend
- our neighbour.

Tautology

Overuse of adjectives and adverbs often leads to tautology – unnecessary repetition.

Do not, for example, write:

- return back – 'return' means to go or to give back so the adverb 'back' is tautological
- ascend up – 'ascend' means to go up
- reply back – 'reply' means to speak or write back.

> **TOP TIP**
> As you revise, make your own list of common tautologies to avoid.

Exercise

Work out what is wrong with this sentence which appeared recently in a newspaper:

President Chen says the government of Taiwan plans to re-apply for UN membership again in the future.

Paragraphing

A paragraph is, of course, a group of sentences within a piece of prose writing (i.e. not poetry or a play) that are grouped together and separated from the rest of the writing. A paragraph can sometimes consist of a single sentence and occasionally – usually for dramatic effect – a single word.

Begin a new paragraph when:

- you introduce a new topic, idea, character or opinion
- a new person speaks in a passage of dialogue in a story
- you want to create a dramatic effect.

Remember:

- in modern writing long, wandering paragraphs are generally regarded as weak style (although 19th century writers such as Jane Austen and Charles Dickens loved them); three or four sentences is usually an ideal
- good paragraphing shows the examiner that you can organise your ideas in writing – which is one of the main things looked for in this exam
- if in doubt, begin a new paragraph
- a one-sentence or even a one-word paragraph can be a useful way of making your writing dramatic.

5.2 Writing stories

One of the options in Paper 2 is usually to write a story. This requires some thought before you start about how the story will begin, develop and end, and the style in which you will write. The section on creating characters (see page 62) will also help you to write a good story.

Plan your story

Plan your story so that you know where it's going. Never try, in an exam, to make up a story as you go along. Spend about 5 minutes creating your plan.

For example, if you were asked to write a story which begins with a telephone conversation, your plan might look like this:

1.   Mother and TV presenter talking on the phone. Competition results. Child has won trip to Antarctica.

2.   Mother off phone – her feelings.

3.   Flashback to advertisement for the competition and entering it. Child's very strong ambition to see Antarctica.

4.   Some time later. Setting off for the trip – airport. Meeting rest of group. Excitement.

Once you have an outline plan of your story, you can fill in the details as you write. For the example above, you would need to think about the following:

● Is the child a boy or a girl?

● How old is he/she?

● What is his/her name?

● What did entering the competition involve?

● Why is he/she keen to go to Antarctica? Has he/she read a lot about it or seen television documentaries? Was his/her great-great-grandparent an explorer?

Exercise

Try the sample question above for yourself. Either use the plan given or devise a completely different plan of your own. Allow yourself about 30 minutes' writing time.

Beginnings and endings

Think for a moment about any traditional fairy story. It begins 'Once upon a time ...' and it ends 'And they all lived happily ever after.' Anything that happens between these is the middle of the story.

Your story will, almost certainly, be more complex than a fairy story, but the examiner is still looking for an effective opening and a rounded-off ending. Think of these as the frame which encloses your story.

There are many ways of starting a story. For example, you can:

- Introduce a character. For example:

  Fergus was sitting on the sea wall idly drumming his heels …

- Set the scene. For example:

  The bell rang and Year 6 erupted noisily through the damp, grey walled area into the panelled hall where hot chocolate and buns awaited them …

- Describe a situation in which everything is not quite what it seems, to tantalise your reader. Then in the next paragraph you explain what is really happening. For example:

  They were being attacked on all sides. The noise rattled over their heads. Adrenaline had never been higher. This was life and death … James and Abdullah had always loved football. It was what cemented their friendship …

- Jump straight into unexplained dialogue and later explain who is speaking and why. For example:

  'Let's go inside and find out.'

  'Do you really think we should?'

  'Yes, come on.'

  Hannah and Jessica were standing outside Horniman's Museum in London. Hannah was insisting that one of the exhibits was a famous stuffed walrus. Jessica was sceptical.

- Make a mysterious statement to entice the reader read on. For example:

  It was all Shakespeare's fault …

  I have always adored apricot jam …

Exercise

Write five opening paragraphs, one for each of the five methods explained above.

- Another way to begin, if you find it very difficult to write a complete story in just over half an hour, is to imagine that you are writing two or three pages from the *middle* of an exciting, gripping, interesting or moving book.

  This means you don't have to worry so much about balanced and satisfying beginnings and endings. You can concentrate instead on making your writing as lively as possible.

  If you decide to do this in your exam:

  - plan your writing just as carefully as if you were producing a complete story
  - state clearly at the top that this is a passage extracted from an imaginary book
  - give your imagined novel a title
  - write a one or two sentence introduction at the top similar to the explanations teachers and examiners put in front of passages taken from books for comprehension work
  - try to end on an exciting 'cliff hanger' to tantalise the reader.

You can end your story in different ways too. For instance, you might:

- Spring a surprise. End with something the reader was not expecting. For example, if two characters have been exploring a cave your reader is probably waiting for them to discover something interesting and come out safe at the end. Instead you could drown them as the tide comes in. If you write a love story you might end with the two people separating without the obvious 'happy ever after' ending.

- Take your characters back to where they started. So, for example, have your character sitting on the sea wall at the end of the story as he was at the beginning.

- End with a joke. For example:

  The moral of this story is that parents are better news than you might think.

  And so, you see, it isn't usually a good idea to pit yourself against a challenge – whatever teachers, pushy parents and youth leaders might tell you.

Avoid the following:

- Endings that have been done far too often before and will make the examiner sigh in exasperation. For example, the narrator waking up at the end and revealing it was all a dream, or revealing that the mystery character sighted earlier (perhaps on a roadside) is the ghost of someone who died there a while ago.

- Tailing off without a definite ending.

> **TOP TIP**
>
> Strong beginnings and endings almost always mean a well-written, gripping story likely to attract high marks in an examination.

Using the first or third person

Most stories are told by:

- an invisible narrator who describes from the outside what is happening to characters and refers to them as 'he', 'she' or 'they' – known grammatically as the third person

- a character who is part of the story him or herself so there is an 'I' – or first person – in the story.

Before you start to write your story, you must decide whether you are going to write it in the first person or the third person.

Even if you opt for the third person you are quite likely to present what happens through the eyes of one character.

Once you have made up your mind who is telling your story, it is essential that you stick to it. Stories which begin in the third person and then slip into the first by mistake go badly wrong and lose many marks.

Exercise

Write two paragraphs from different stories, one in the first person and the other in the third.

5.3 Creating characters

There are some key points to remember when creating your characters and writing their dialogue.

Interesting characters

Make sure your story includes some colourful characters but do not try to include too many. Although some novels have dozens of characters, the story that you write in your exam will be very short so you do not have space for more than two or three main characters. If you try to include more, your story will be confused and confusing.

Present each character in as much detail as you can. Show him or her doing and saying things as a way of communicating to your reader what the character is like. This is usually more effective than just telling the reader what the character is like.

In each of these examples, the first option is more effective than the second:

1. Sophie was curled up on the settee reading *David Copperfield* by Charles Dickens.
2. Sophie is an intelligent girl who loves books.

1. As Jake opened his birthday card from his grandmother, a cheque for £500 fell on to the floor.
2. Jake's grandmother is very well off.

Characters' names

Give the characters in your story believable names. In real life a person's name is usually related to one or more of the following:

- The period in which he or she was born. In the early 20th century many babies were given names such as Albert, Doris, Phyllis and Vera. In the middle of the 20th century Susan, David, Peter and Anne were popular. By the 1990s, it was Oliver, Chloe, Charlotte and Ben. Some names, of course, move in and out of fashion. Old names such as George, Henry, Florence and Beatrice are popular again now.

- The country he or she comes from. Names such as Callum and Douglas are often Scottish. Huw and Gwyneth are Welsh names. Names such as Eva, Elena and Nicolas (spelt without the 'h') are popular in many European countries.

> **TOP TIP**
> Learn **SCIA** (**S**how **C**haracters **i**n **A**ction) and keep it in mind as you write your story.

- His or her social class. In the early 20th century someone called Violet was more likely to be a servant than a girl named Alexandra. A boy named Ron was more likely to work in, say, a coalmine, than a young man called Julian.

Your story will ring much truer if you give your characters appropriate names. Think about the names of the people you know – the very elderly, the middle-aged, younger people and anyone you know who comes (or whose family comes) from outside Britain.

Dialogue

Dialogue can be used to show what characters are like too. Let your characters introduce themselves to your reader through what they say. This is what happens in real life and so it works well in stories.

Look, for example, at how the caring, respectful side of Hazel's character is shown in the words he uses in this extract. Note that Hazel is a rabbit, speaking to his brother, Fiver:

> *'You don't suppose I'll leave you to look after yourself, do you?' said Hazel. 'But to tell you the truth, I sometimes feel like clearing out of this warren altogether. Still, let's forget it now and try to enjoy the evening. I'll tell you what — shall we go across the brook? There'll be fewer rabbits there and we can have a bit of peace. Unless you feel it isn't safe?' he added.*
>
> (From *Watership Down* by Richard Adams, 1972)

Here's another example which is written as a first person narrative. Look at how much you learn about the narrator from what the author makes her say here, near the beginning of the book:

> *I checked my nails, smoothed down my pinafore and sniffed. I was not used to being right inside the house and the air seemed to close about me stiflingly, an inside sort of air, stuffy and tickling my nose, a mixture of the previous night's coal fires, the fibres of the thick wool carpets and the scent from the bowl of dried rose petals on the hall table.*
>
> (From *The Disgrace of Kitty Grey* by Mary Hooper, 2013)

Exercise

Write a paragraph or two of dialogue in which your character or characters begin to reveal what they think or feel or what their personalities are like.

When you are writing dialogue try to make it more interesting and less repetitive by using words other than 'said' to explain who is speaking. There are many other possibilities, some of them quite colourful, such as:

whispered	asked	muttered
grumbled	bellowed	breathed
suggested	growled	demanded
enquired	proposed	groaned
questioned	exclaimed	shouted
murmured	declaimed	mumbled

TOP TIP

As part of your revision, create a list of words to use when you are writing dialogue. Add to the list any words for 'said' you come across in your reading.

Sometimes, if two characters are speaking alternately in short sentences, you don't need explanatory words to tell the reader who is speaking. This has the effect of making the dialogue run very fast down the page and is good, for example, for arguments.

For example:

> 'Look what I've got,' she said, waving it at me, like a baby-faced assassin.
> 'What is it like?'
> 'What does it look like?
> 'And where did you find it?'
> 'Sue gave it to me.'
> It felt so good to be having a conversation with her ….
>
> (From *Firewallers* by Simon Packham, 2013)

5.4 Writing descriptions

In Paper 2 you are often given the option to write a description – or the freedom to treat a subject in any way you like.

A description is, for the purposes of this exam, a piece of imaginative writing which describes, say, a person, place or event without the full plot you'd create in a story.

For example, if you were given the subject 'the beach' and decided to write a description rather than a story you might imagine and write about:

- a lonely, sandy beach along a bay at dawn
- the smell and sounds
- huge waves
- two surfers arriving in the distance and starting to ride the waves
- one man with a dog on the beach
- seabirds searching for worms
- ships out at sea
- the atmosphere including the light.

Or, if you wanted to write a description in response to the subject 'the old man', you might simply create a character and describe him as if you were introducing him to the reader.
You might describe his:

- appearance
- manner
- home
- dog
- family
- background
- likes and dislikes
- habits.

You should be sure to make him as unusual and interesting as possible.

> **TOP TIP**
> Remember that almost all stories and novels use description as part of the storytelling. The descriptions are woven into the text alongside dialogue. If you write a description in your exam, think of it as an extract from a novel.

Beginning

You should begin your writing with a strong statement which will make your reader want to read on. For example:

- My Uncle Joe is a puppeteer.
- Everyone in my family has childhood memories of Bournemouth since my great-great-grandfather bought a holiday home there in 1921.
- I was in the water. It was deep and cold. I was fully dressed. There was no one in sight.

Using your senses

Use all five of your senses to bring your writing to life. Write about what you can:

- hear, for example the waves on that beach
- smell, for example the seaweed
- taste, for example the salt on your lips
- feel, for example the sand beneath your feet
- see – this is the most obvious one.

Using your memories

Use your memories and make them as entertaining as you can. You might, for example, remember a special holiday, visiting a relative or a time when something interesting, funny, sad or silly happened to you.

Using metaphors and similes

Use interesting – and original – metaphors and similes. They will make your writing more vivid, exciting and memorable.

In each of these examples, the first option is more effective than the second:

❶ She felt as if she was standing on the edge of a perilous precipice.
❷ She was scared.

❶ I fell upon my food like a starving hyena.
❷ I ate my lunch hungrily.

❶ My mother is an inspired and enthusiastic artist in the kitchen, mixing a fabulous palate of tastes and textures in her pans and pots.
❷ My mother is a good cook.

5.5 Practice tasks

This is an example of the choice you can expect in Paper 2 Section B. Use the tasks for practice.

You should spend around 40 minutes in total on each task. Spend the first 5 minutes planning. Write for about 30 minutes. Read your work through in the last 5 minutes to check for mistakes and to make small changes.

1. Write a story or a description using one of the following titles:

    (a) A surprise

    (b) The visit to the castle

    (c) Shopping

2. 'It is never too late.'
    Write about this in any imaginative way you wish.

3. 'Did you do this?'
    'Yes and I'll tell you why.'
    Write a story which includes these two lines of dialogue.

4. Reaching the top

Chapter 6: Grammar, punctuation and spelling

Your 13+ English exams involve reading carefully, writing perceptive answers and producing imaginative or well-reasoned essays.

A sound knowledge of the basic 'nuts and bolts' of English will help you to do all of that with precision.

Usually grammar, punctuation and spelling are not marked separately – although some senior schools choose to give a separate mark out of 10 for grammar which often includes punctuation and spelling. This would mean that if you write imaginatively and have a good vocabulary but have, for example, a spelling learning difficulty the examiner will give you the marks you deserve for your ideas without being put off by your spelling.

In most cases, however, your grammar, punctuation and spelling are marked along with the content you write. It is part of the general impression your work gives the examiner – and an important part.

You will **not** be asked specific questions about grammar (or punctuation or spelling) in your papers.

> **TOP TIP**
> Pay close attention to grammar, punctuation and spelling because they underpin everything you write. Just as a building will collapse if its foundations are not properly built so your writing may be seriously weakened by poor grammar, punctuation and spelling.

> **TOP TIP**
> Revise the technicalities of English thoroughly so that you make as few mistakes as possible in your writing. Errors will cost you marks.

6.1 Word classes or 'parts of speech'

There are at least two good reasons for knowing the main word classes:

- If you have good background knowledge of the shape of sentences and the different sorts of words which go into a good one you are more likely to be able to construct sentences which convey their meaning clearly and effectively.

- It can be useful to use the vocabulary of grammar in a comprehension answer. You might write for example:

    ★ The poet's use of aggressive verbs …
    ★ The effect of the author's list of abstract nouns suggests …

Here is a brief summary of the parts of speech and how they work. There is more detail – if you need it – in *So you really want to learn English* Books 1, 2 and 3.

Remember that words are not loyal. They belong to different groups depending on the job they are required to do in a particular sentence. So concentrate on what sort of a word it is in the sentence you are writing or studying. Don't worry about what sort of word it might be in a different context.

Nouns

A noun is a naming word. There are several sorts.

- Common – for example:

    chair, computer, house, boy

- Proper – for example:

    Edinburgh, Prince Harry, Pizza Express, River Mersey

- Abstract – for example:

    adoration, anger, thirst, carelessness

- Collective – for example:

    herd (of cattle), pack (of cards), flock (of birds or sheep).

TOP TIP

Try to revise one of the eight parts of speech covered here each day. Make up more examples as part of your revision. Tick off each word class when you are sure you have learnt it.

Verbs

Verbs are the action or 'being' words which show you what is happening in a sentence.

- ★ We **walked** all the way to town.
- ★ Mr Smith **is** our teacher.
- ★ '**Run** faster!' **shouted** the cricket coach.
- ★ We **are** the champions.

Verbs can be expressed in various versions of the past, present and future tenses, depending on when the action or situation took, takes, or will take, place.

In sentences verbs often consist of several words because they sometimes use auxiliary (helping) verbs – to have or to be – to show the tense.

- ★ In October we **shall have been living** in our house for ten years.
- ★ I **was wandering** along the corridor.
- ★ You **will be** late for school.
- ★ **Has** she **been reading** *Harry Potter and the Philosopher's Stone?*

Adjectives

Adjectives are describing words which 'qualify' or 'modify' – or tell you more about – nouns.

- ★ I love **hot**, **sunny summer** days.
- ★ Drink your tea before it gets **cold**.
- ★ **Red** roses are my **favourite** flowers.

They can be used in a comparative (more) form:

    hotter, more exciting, better

Or a superlative (most) form:

    hottest, most exciting, best

Adverbs

Adverbs are describing words which 'qualify' or 'modify' – or tell you more about – verbs.

They usually tell you how, when, where or why something happens.

- ★ Oliver Twist and his friends ate **hungrily**.
- ★ My horse **rapidly** overtook hers.
- ★ Let's do it **now**.
- ★ Snow lay **everywhere**.

Adverbs also sometimes qualify other adverbs or adjectives.

- ★ The girl was **unusually** small.
- ★ We thought it was best to get there **quite** quickly.

> **TOP TIP**
>
> Think of an adverb as an add-verb because it **adds** to the meaning of the **verb**, but be careful to spell **adverb** correctly**.**

Pronouns

Pronouns stand in the place of nouns. They mean you don't have to keep clumsily repeating the nouns in your sentences.

There are several sorts:

- Personal

  I, you, he, she, it, we, they (when it's the subject of the verb). For example:

  - ★ **He** and **I** went swimming.

  him, her, it, us, them (when it's the object or 'receiver' of the verb). For example:

  - ★ Mrs Wentworth told **us** what to do.

- Demonstrative – this dog, that pencil. Such pronouns often drop the accompanying noun. For example:

  - ★ That pencil is sharp.
  - ★ That is sharp.

- Possessive – my, mine, your, yours, his, her, hers, its, our, ours, their, theirs. For example:

  - ★ **His** book is very absorbing.
  - ★ The book is **his**.
  - ★ The building is **our** house.
  - ★ The house is **ours**.

- Relative – who, which, whom, whose. For example:

  - ★ My cousin, **whom** you don't know, lives in Cornwall.
  - ★ This is the book **which** I was telling you about.

  In these examples the pronoun stands for 'my cousin' and 'the book'.

Take particular care with 'who' and 'whom'.

- 'Whom' is used when it is standing as the object of a verb or when it follows prepositions (for example to, by, of, through, from, by, at).

  We use 'whom' when, in a differently structured variation of the sentence, we would use 'him' (not 'he').

  For example:

  ★ This is the man **whom** my sister loves. (she loves **him**.)
  ★ This is the teacher from **whom** I learnt French last year. (I learnt it from **him**.)
  ★ This is the boy with **whom** I went on a Scout camp. (I went with **him**.)
  ★ To **whom** does this pencil case belong? (does it belong to **him**?)

- 'Who' is used when it is standing as the subject of the verb. We use 'who' when, in other circumstances, we would say 'he'.

  For example:

  ★ This is the man **who** loves my sister. (**he** loves her.)
  ★ This is the teacher **who** taught me French last year. (**he** taught me.)
  ★ This is the boy **who** went with me on a Scout camp. (**he** went with me.)
  ★ **Who** owns this pencil case? (**he** owns it.)

Prepositions

Prepositions tell you the **position** of something in relation to something else.

> **TOP TIP**
> Think of prepositions as place words – p for place and p for preposition.

- ★ The jam is **in** the cupboard.
- ★ **Under** the apple tree Felix is asleep.
- ★ The dish ran away **with** the spoon.

Other prepositions include: within, inside, outside, over, beneath, above, around, up, down, into, with, at.

But many of these words can, as so often in English, also be used to do other jobs in sentences when they are not being prepositions. For more help with this see the section on 'Words doing many jobs' on p.71.

Conjunctions

Conjunctions are joining words.

> **TOP TIP**
> To remember what conjunctions do, think of the **junction** on a railway where two or more lines join.

They can be used to join short sentences to create longer ones or sometimes to hook words together.

Common everyday conjunctions include: and, or, because, as, although, but, though, so.

For example:

- ★ The prize went jointly to Marina **and** Oliver.
- ★ I like peas **and** so does my brother. (I like peas. My brother does too.)

★ I am going fishing at the weekend **because** it is my favourite activity. (I am going fishing at the weekend. It is my favourite activity.)

Like prepositions, conjunctions are slippery little words. The same words often get into sentences doing other jobs. Look, as ever, at *how* they are used before you decide what they are.

Articles

- 'The' is the definite article and refers to something specific. For example:

  ★ **the** government
  ★ **the** sea.

Each of these refers to a specific one.

- 'A' is the indefinite article. For example:

  ★ **a** fox
  ★ **a** poem.

These are not specific because they refer to any fox or poem.

- 'An' is a form of the indefinite article used when the next word begins with a vowel. For example:

  ★ **an** elephant
  ★ **an** apple
  ★ **an** old coat.

Words doing many jobs

Some words can act as different parts of speech in different sentences.

Take the word 'up', for example:

- Where is the **up** escalator? (adjective)
- We all have our ups and downs and just now I'm enjoying an **up**. (noun)
- The village is **up** there. (preposition)
- I often walk **up** steps because it is good exercise. (adverb)

> **TOP TIP**
> Try writing a number of short sentences (which follow on logically from each other). Then join them all up into one long sentence, using conjunctions. For example: 'I don't like broccoli. I eat it. It's good for me.' There are several ways you could organise this into one long sentence.

> **TOP TIP**
> The best way of really making sure you have grasped something is to teach it to someone else.

Exercise

Try using these words as different parts of speech in different sentences: break, fast, as, set, down – and/or think of some other words that you could use in this way. Then try explaining what you've done to someone who doesn't quite understand it.

6.2 Punctuation

This is a summary of the most important uses of the main punctuation marks used in English.

It's important to get your punctuation right, because punctuation marks can change the meaning of a sentence so incorrect punctuation can confuse your examiner.

Ending a sentence

- End every sentence with a full stop (.)

  Sometimes it is appropriate to use a question mark (?) or exclamation mark (!) both of which include a full stop.

  Do **not** end a sentence with a comma.

  Study these two extracts from Ernest Hemingway's short story *Indian Camp* for correct use of the full stop as a sentence ending. Notice how short some of the sentences are:

> *The two boats started off in the dark. Nick heard the oar-locks of the other boat quite a long way ahead of them in the mist. The Indians rowed with short choppy strokes. Nick lay back with his father's arm around him. It was cold on the water.*
>
> *…*
>
> *Across the bay they found the other boat beached. Uncle George was smoking a cigar in the dark. The young Indian pulled the boat way up the beach. Uncle George gave both the Indians cigars.*

- Use a question mark if a question is being asked. For example:
  - ★ How far is it to York?
  - ★ Are we nearly there?

- Use an exclamation mark if you want to turn something you've written into a joke or to make an exclamation dramatic. For example:
  - ★ Help!
  - ★ Oh my goodness!

Generally it is bad style, and lazy, to use exclamation marks other than very occasionally.

If your choice of words is strong enough, exclamation marks are usually unnecessary. Think how rarely you see them in newspapers, information books or in good novels (except sometimes in dialogue).

Commas

Commas are used inside sentences. Their job is to make meaning clear.

- They mark a natural break in the sentence or they separate one part of it from another part. For example:
  - ★ Abdul, bring me your homework.
  - ★ Put that parcel over there, please.
  - ★ A tall man, Mr Smith pulled the book from the top shelf.

- They are used to separate items in a list within a sentence. For example:
  - ★ Dogs, cats, guinea pigs, hamsters and rabbits all make good pets.
  - ★ I've read three books by Dickens, two by Jane Austen, two by Elizabeth Gaskell and one by Thomas Hardy.
  - ★ Excited, nervous, exhilarated and passionate, she burst through the door.
- Commas are also used in pairs to separate an aside from the main thrust of the sentence. For example:
  - ★ It is unlikely, however, to happen.
  - ★ Nick Wilkins, a professor of English, told the group about studying the subject at university.
  - ★ Adela, who is new to our school, is outstanding at maths.

Colons

- The colon means 'as follows' or 'like this'. We often use it in this book to follow the words 'for example'. It often precedes lists.
  - ★ These are my favourite animals: panda, zebra and hippopotamus.
  - ★ This is my opinion: private individuals should not be allowed to own guns.
- The colon is not followed by a capital letter unless the word happens to require a capital letter.

Semi-colons

- The semi-colon can be used in long complicated lists between commas for clarity.
  - ❶ Here is a simple list:

    I bought apples, bananas, oranges and plums.

  - ❷ Use semi-colons to expand it into a much longer sentence like this:

    I bought apples, both green and red because we all like different types; bananas which are Dad's favourite, although they sometimes give him indigestion; several sorts of orange, including navels, blood, satsumas and mandarins, and plums.

- Semi-colons can also be used in place of commas or full stops for additional emphasis. For example, see the extract on page 12 from *Set in Stone* by Linda Newbery.

Speech marks

Also sometimes called inverted commas or quotation marks (" " or ' '), speech marks always work in pairs. They separate a group of spoken or quoted words from the rest of the sentence.

- A capital letter is used each time speech marks are opened unless the speaker is in the middle of a sentence. For example:
  - ★ The headmistress said, 'Let us pray.'
  - ★ 'Don't you think,' continued Mary, 'that we should ask permission first?'

- A comma is usually used at the end of the spoken words inside the speech marks before the writer explains who is speaking. For example:
  - ★ 'Let's go,' said James.
  - ★ 'That's very interesting,' observed Latifa.

- If a full stop, question mark or exclamation mark comes at the end of a spoken sentence it goes inside the speech marks. For example:
  - ★ 'Really?' asked Alex.
  - ★ 'Wow!' breathed Niamh.

- A new paragraph begins each time a different character speaks. Study this piece of dialogue as a way of revising speech marks:

> 'Mr Farrow?' he repeated. 'And he, I assume, has sent you to find me for some reason?'
>
> 'No,' I assured him. 'I have come of my own accord. I am a great admirer of your work, Mr Waring – indeed I am fascinated by it.'
>
> He nodded, seeming to accept this as his due.
>
> 'I have been curious to meet you,' I continued, 'from the first time I set eyes on your wind carvings.'
>
> (From *Set in Stone* by Linda Newbery, 2006)

- It doesn't matter whether you use single speech marks (' ') or doubles (" ") but you must be consistent.

- If you need to use speech marks within a passage that is itself in speech marks use the type that you have not already used. This gives one of the following patterns:

  'Bla bla "bla bla" bla bla.'

  "Bla bla 'bla bla' bla bla."

Study this example:

> 'And another thing.' The admiral was still leaning forward. 'Your dossier contains at least one factual error. Clive didn't "surface conveniently installed in my household" … Nash approached me about taking Clive as a replacement, giving him the highest – well "praise" would be more accurate than "endorsement" or "recommendation" … That was twelve years ago.'
>
> (From *The Secret of the Lost Planet* by Mel Hogan, 2007)

Apostrophes

The apostrophe has two uses. It shows:

- possession
- that letters have been missed out (omission).

Possession

- When the possessor is singular the apostrophe goes before the 's':
  - ★ Bernard's dog is the dog possessed by Bernard (one boy – singular).
  - ★ A term's work is the work connected with, or possessed by, the term (one term – singular).

- When the possessor noun is plural the apostrophe goes after the 's'.
  - ★ The girls' changing room is the changing room used, or possessed, by the girls (more than one girl – plural).
  - ★ Three years' effort is an effort lasting, or possessed by, three years (more than one year – plural).

- Take care with words which already end in s or ss in their singular or plural form. Exactly the same rules apply:
  - ★ The duchess's dress (singular)
  - ★ Three actresses' autographs (plural)
  - ★ Brahms's first symphony (singular)
  - ★ Mr Watts's class (singular).

- Note that plural nouns which do not end in s – such as children and women – behave as if they were singular and take an apostrophe before the s when they are possessive. For example:
  - ★ working men's club
  - ★ children's games.

Omission

- The apostrophe may also stand in place of missing letters in contracted words such as:
  - ★ wouldn't (would not)
  - ★ o'clock (of the clock)
  - ★ shan't (shall not)
  - ★ C'bury (Canterbury – on road signs)
  - ★ it's (it is or it has).

Learn this example as part of your revision:

It's a pity that our classroom has its door so close to the street.

> **TOP TIP**
> Be particularly careful with its (which means belonging to it) and it's (which means it is or it has).

Not using the apostrophe

Getting the apostrophe right is partly the art of knowing when **not** to use one.

An 's' at the end of a word usually shows that it is a plural noun and does not need an apostrophe. For example:

- ★ three towns
- ★ four dogs
- ★ two sticks.

or that it is part of a verb, for example:

- ★ he says
- ★ she runs
- ★ Paul sobs.

None of these needs an apostrophe.

No apostrophe is needed anywhere in a sentence like this:

> All the boys in classes one, two and three enjoy basketball lessons but Jules Atkins insists that he prefers card games.

TOP TIP

Remember that far more words do **not** need an apostrophe than need one. Do your best to learn how the apostrophe is used and get it right in your exam. But if in doubt leave it out. You will make fewer mistakes that way.

Capital (or upper case) letters

Every sentence should begin with a capital letter.

Most capital letters are larger than the other letters in a word – make the distinction clearly, especially when the two forms are the same, or similar, shape such as Cc, Ss or Kk.

Many capital letters are a different shape from the lower case letter, such as Mm or Dd. Some, like Pp and Jj, have a different position on the line. Pay attention to this so that the examiner does not think you are misusing capital letters. If it looks to someone who is unfamiliar with your writing as though you are failing to begin sentences and proper nouns with capitals you will lose marks.

You also normally need an upper case or capital letter:

- For all proper nouns. For example:

  Estella Jones, Bridgewood Preparatory School, Bristol, River Dee, Tesco.

- At the beginning of most lines of poetry. For example:

  Slowly, silently now the moon
  Walks the night in her silver shoon.

- Usually for the first word inside inverted commas.
  For example:

  Dick said, 'And I'll come too,' when he saw us getting ready.

- For most initials and acronyms. For example:

  NATO, RSPCA

TOP TIP

Sometimes handwriting makes it difficult to tell whether a letter is lower or upper case (small or capital). Make sure your writing is not guilty of this. Get out of bad habits if you need to.

6.3 Grammar

Grammar is a big subject and you will by now have studied the details carefully in your English lessons.

This section cannot cover the whole of English grammar, but here are some important things to revise and remember.

Agreement of subject and verb

Every sentence has a subject. It may be one word such as 'I' or 'Katie'. It may be something more complex such as 'Mr Patterson, our popular and witty Year 8 teacher'.

The subject often comes at the beginning of the sentence, but it doesn't have to.

Not far from the subject of any sentence is a verb – the action performed by the subject or the state the subject is in.

The sentence may have other things too, but a subject and a verb are the basic building bricks.

It is important to make sure that your subject and verb agree. A singular subject needs a singular verb. If the subject is plural then, of course, it needs a plural verb.

This is pretty straightforward in sentences such as:

- ★ I **danced**.
- ★ Katie **shouted** at the top of her voice.
- ★ Mr Patterson, our popular and witty year 8 teacher, **retires** this year.

But be careful in sentences like this:

- ★ The weather, the miserable surroundings and the poor facilities **were** all responsible for our unsuccessful holiday. (Plural subject: 'The weather, the miserable surroundings and the poor facilities').
- ★ Everyone **is** here. (Singular subject 'everyone'.)

Take care too with collective nouns. They are singular:

- ★ The Labour Party **is** planning its next election campaign.
- ★ The choir **is** waiting for its conductor.
- ★ The pride of lions **sleeps** most of the day.

> **TOP TIP**
>
> If there are any other points of grammar that you are not sure about after you have worked through this section then look at *So you really want to learn English* Book 2 or 3. Or ask a teacher to help you.

> **TOP TIP**
>
> Note that these words are all singular and need singular verbs to agree with them:
>
> | | |
> |---|---|
> | anybody | everybody |
> | nobody | anyone |
> | each | everyone |
> | everything | either |
> | neither | none |
>
> For example:
>
> - ★ **Neither** of the men **was** guilty.
> - ★ We lost several tennis balls but **none was** found.
> - ★ **Each** of the twenty quizzes **was** harder than the one before.

Clauses and phrases

Clauses and phrases are groups of words within sentences.

A clause has a verb of its own. For example:

★ A nurse **she <u>had not seen</u> before** came and sat on the edge of her bed.

★ And I knew that one day **when I <u>was</u> bigger** I would become one of the top men.

★ We were in a small room **which <u>held</u> nothing except a large grating in the stone floor**.

A clause usually adds extra detail to the main sentence, but if you remove it the sentence should still make sense. Try it with the examples above.

A phrase is two or more words used together in a sentence. It does not include a verb. It can be a word group of almost any shape. For example:

★ We followed him **through the house** until we reached the kitchen.

★ They had seen the film **earlier that evening**.

★ **Given the choice** I like fantasy stories best.

★ Simon set out **wearing full climbing gear**.

★ **Ladies and gentleman**, I have an announcement to make.

> **TOP TIP**
> Remember that good sentences consist of varying patterns of clauses and phrases woven together.

Ten mistakes to avoid in your English

Work through these – perhaps study one a day for a few minutes.

Then tick them off when you've practised and understood them.

1. I and me

Don't confuse 'I' with 'me' when you put it with another person.

'I' is usually the subject in the sentence or clause and 'me' the object (direct or indirect). If in doubt remove the other person from the sentence and work out what you would write if you were using the pronoun on its own.

So, you should write:

★ Jonathan and **I** played cricket. (**I** played cricket.)

★ She gave him and **me** a telling off. (She gave **me** a telling off.)

★ Good night from her and **me**. (Good night from **me**.)

★ My twin sister and **I** are 12 years old. (**I** am 12 years old.)

> **TOP TIP**
> Me and Tony went fishing … is *always* wrong.
> Dad gave Charlotte and I ten pounds each … is *always* wrong.

2. Himself, herself, myself, yourself

Do not use 'himself' or 'herself', or 'myself' or 'yourself', as the subject (or part of the subject) of a sentence.

* ★ Sarah and I have … is correct.
* ★ Sarah and myself have … is **always** wrong.

3. Too, to and two

* ★ I am **too** tall for these trousers. (too much of something)
* ★ Alex wanted to come **too**. (as well)
* ★ She ate **two** ice creams. (number)
* ★ May I have permission **to** go **to** the school office? (all other uses)

TOP TIP

Learn this sentence to help you remember too, to and two:

Two boys, **too** curious for their own good, ran **to** the cupboard **to** look inside.

4. Two words or one?

Strictly speaking, 'all right' is two separate words, 'all' and 'right'. The form 'alright' is often seen, and is similar to the forms 'altogether' and 'already', but is considered bad form in formal writing.

But learn the difference between all ready/already.

In this example, 'ready' is an adjective telling you more about 'we' and 'all' is a separate adverb telling you more about 'ready':

* ★ Are we all ready to go?

In this example, 'already' is an adverb meaning 'in good time':

* ★ He has arrived already.

Similarly, 'thank you' is two words. So is 'a lot'.

TOP TIP

Work out the difference in meaning between 'altogether' and 'all together'.

5. Less, few and fewer

Less refers to quantity. For example:

* ★ less salt
* ★ less rainfall
* ★ less hope

Fewer or few refer to a number. For example:

* ★ fewer eggs
* ★ few people
* ★ few schools

A quick way of remembering this is that if it's something you can count (eggs, people, houses) it is 'few' or 'fewer'. If you can't count it, use 'less'.

TOP TIP

Some British supermarkets have a notice up saying 'Baskets containing fewer than eight items' – which is correct. Several other supermarkets get this wrong. Watch out for it. The more aware you are, the *fewer* mistakes you will make yourself.

6. Lie and lay

Learn that 'to lie' is a verb meaning either to put oneself in a horizontal position or to tell untruths. For example:

★ I lie on the bed when I am tired.
★ I lie to get myself out of difficult situations.

The past tense for the first meaning is 'lay' or 'have lain'. For example:

★ I lay on the grass all day yesterday.
★ I have lain on the grass all morning and now it's time for lunch.

TOP TIP

On Sundays (if you're lucky) you might enjoy a lie-in – and it is an error to call it anything else.

The untruth sense is easier. The past tense is 'lied' or 'have lied'. For example:

★ I lied to him yesterday because I have always lied to him.

The verb 'to lay' is used when the person carrying out the action (the verb's subject) is doing something to something else (technically known as a transitive verb). For example:

★ You can lay eggs (if you happen to be a hen), bricks, carpets or tables.

The past tense is 'laid' or 'have laid'. For example:

★ freshly laid eggs
★ well-laid table.

Remember we're dealing with three different verbs here. Make sure you understand the difference so that you don't muddle them.

7. Only, and other adverbs

It is important to put the word 'only' in the correct place in a sentence. Getting it wrong (as many people do) changes the meaning. Study these examples:

★ Only we saw the play that afternoon. (No one else saw it.)
★ We saw only the play that afternoon. (We didn't see anything else.)
★ We only saw the play that afternoon. (We didn't, for example, read it or rehearse it.)
★ We saw the play only that afternoon. (We saw it very recently.)

Take care with the positioning of other adverbs such as 'even', 'always' and 'often' too. These two sentences do not mean quite the same thing:

★ We even went swimming.
★ Even we went swimming.

The first sentence suggests that there were lots of interesting things to do including swimming. The second implies that many people were swimming so, although it was unusual for us, we did too.

Compare these two sentences:

★ She often went to the cinema on Fridays.
★ She went to the cinema, often on Fridays.

The first sentence means that usually, every Friday, she went to the cinema. The second means that she frequently went to the cinema on various days of the week, often choosing Fridays.

8. Practice and practise

Practice with a 'c' is a noun:

★ I must do some clarinet practice.

★ Practice is important if you want to improve your tennis.

★ Dr Ahmed's medical practice covered three villages.

Sometimes it becomes an adjective:

★ The practice rooms are at the back of the music room.

★ The hour before supper is cricket practice time.

Practise with an 's' is a verb:

★ I must practise the clarinet.

★ Practise your tennis if you want to improve.

★ Dr Ahmed and his colleagues practise in three villages.

Use **advice** and **advise** to help you remember this. They are easier because they sound different. Say aloud:

★ Here is my advice. (noun)

★ We could try the advice centre. (adjective)

★ I advise you to apologise. (verb)

★ She advised me to come. (verb)

Licence/license and **prophecy/prophesy** follow the same pattern.

Be aware that in American English these words are always spelled with a 'c' even when they are verbs.

9. Subjects

If you use a phrase or a clause before the subject of your sentence take care that it does not clash with the subject.

For example, do not write the following (it means that you are a wet day!):

★ Being a wet day, I stayed indoors.

You should write one of the following:

★ It was a wet day so I stayed indoors.
★ I stayed indoors because it was a wet day.

Do not write the following as it as it sounds as if John is about to take the assembly and then stops talking:

★ Knowing he was ready to begin assembly John stopped talking and listened to the headmaster.

You should write:

★ John stopped talking and listened to the headmaster who was ready to begin the assembly.

10. They're, their and there

'They're' is a short form of they are. For example:

★ They're enjoying the sunshine.

'Their' is a possessive pronoun. For example:

★ The children eat their lunch at 12 o'clock.

'There' can be an adverb. For example:

★ We walked there in half an hour.

'There' can also be a pronoun. For example:

★ Put your bag there.

Study this correct sentence:

As soon as the boys arrive they're expected to put their bags in the lockers over there.

6.4 Spelling

You will have done a lot of work on spelling during English (and perhaps other) lessons over the years. Now, as you revise, it's just a matter of going over the words you know you are likely to get wrong and memorising them.

Once you have really mastered a particular word you are unlikely ever to have a problem with it again. And it usually takes only a minute or two's concentration.

You could work with a partner, testing each other, or you might prefer to work alone. Practise writing the words. Don't spell them aloud. That is a different skill (and a bit more difficult for most people). In your exam you will need to write them so concentrate on that.

One way of practising writing them is to make up a story using as many of the words you have difficulties spelling as possible.

TOP TIP

Incorrect spelling creates a bad impression. Don't just avoid writing a word that you can't spell in an exam, however, as this is a rather lazy solution and it limits your vocabulary. It is much better to spend a little time learning any spellings you don't know. It will help you in other subjects as well as English.

You could arrange the words you need to learn in short lists of five or ten a day.

Here, in alphabetical order, are some of the most commonly misspelt everyday words in English.

Tick each word off if – or when – you are confident that you can spell it:

TOP TIP
Keep a notebook of words you usually get wrong or find difficult and include these in your revision.

absence	disappear	necessary
access	disappoint	neighbour
accommodation	dissatisfy	niece
achieve	eerie	ninety
across	eligible	noticeable
address	exaggerate	occur
advantageous	exceed	occurring
aerial	except	parallel
analyse	excessive	possession
anxious	exhilaration	procedure
arctic	forty	proceed
argument	fulfil	profession
association	gauge	pursue
author	grammatical	queue
autumn	guard	receipt
awkward	handkerchief	receive
beautiful	height	recommend
beginning	holiday	repetition
benefited	humorous	restaurant
biscuit	humour	rhyme
business	immediate	rhythm
ceiling	independent	ridiculous
changeable	install	secretary
commit	instalment	separate
committed	irritable	sincerely
committee	knowledge	solemn
comparison	leisure	success
conceit	library	thorough
condemn	likeable	truly
conscience	lovable	vicious
conscientious	maintenance	weird
coolly	manageable	wholly
deceive	Mediterranean	wilfully
definitely	miscellaneous	yacht
desirable	mischief	yield
despair	mischievous	
development	necessarily	

83

6.5 Summary

You should now know:

- the different word classes or 'parts of speech'
- the main punctuation marks used in English
- the main grammar points to revise
- the ten key things to avoid
- how to spell some of the most commonly misspelt words.

6.6 Test yourself

Make sure you can answer the following questions. See Chapter 7 for the answers.

1.   What is a noun?

2.   What is a verb?

3.   What is an adjective?

4.   What is an adverb?

5.   What is a pronoun?

6.   What is a preposition?

7.   What is a conjunction?

8.   Name the three punctuation marks which can end a sentence.

9.   What are speech marks sometimes called?

10. Put the apostrophes in the correct place in this sentence:
     Its a great shame that the tree has lost its leaves as its Dads favourite.

Chapter 7: Guidance for practice tasks

Please remember that the suggestions here are just examples of the sorts of thing examiners are looking for. They are **not** the single, correct way of answering the questions. English is a very open-ended subject unlike, say, maths.

It might help to think of what you read here as 'notes' to help you to see what the questions, and the passages they relate to, mean and use this learning as part of your revision. In no sense is what follows here intended to be seen as the only correct answers.

7.1 Chapter 2

1. Fiction

Level 1 (The Day of the Triffids)

1. The writer is surprised because he hears a noise he can't at first identify. Then he realises it's a 'normally blind' man with a white stick. (1)

2. The words are: 'Neatly dressed'; 'straightened up, a little defiantly' and 'an exaggerated air of independence'. (3)

    The man is neatly dressed because, unlike the other man who has chosen his tie by feel, as a blind man he is used to dressing himself and can manage it.

    He has evidently disliked being treated as a victim in the past and is now delighted that the rest of the population will need its 'patronage' for itself. He is therefore defiant.

    Once he is told what has happened, and has thought about it, the normally blind man seems rather pleased – giving a 'short bitter laugh' – because he is now the one with the advantages. He walks away from the narrator in a cheerful mood with 'an exaggerated air of independence.' (3)

3. The writer tells us the young man is 'wearing a well-cut suit', although he couldn't choose a matching tie by feel. Second, he knows he has to find a way of getting food. So, he speaks to the woman and uses her child to confirm that there are 'Apples and fings in the shop'. He wouldn't normally steal but accepts that he has to and breaks a shop window to get oranges which he shares fairly with the woman and child. This shows that he knows how to seize an opportunity. (4)

4. The woman has to look after her young child Mary, who whines, has to be carried by her mother and speaks childishly. Yet the mother cannot see and the child can. The mother understands this although the child evidently does not. Second, we can see too from the incident with the oranges, that this child is going to be very valuable to her mother and anyone else she meets. The mother is very reluctant to steal even to eat. (4)

5. 'Why is it so quiet?' and 'stranded vehicles'. (2)

    The 'normally blind' man is puzzled by the quiet. He knows it isn't night because he can feel the sun. He draws attention to the unnatural quiet by asking his question.

We infer from the stranded vehicles that they have been abandoned because suddenly no one can see to drive any more. This would mean an immediate quietness in which sounds such as the tapping of a white stick and the sound of the shop window breaking would be very loud. (4)

6. She is not an educated woman but she knows that 'We didn't ought to take 'em'. But no one can get food in the conventional way so the ordinary rules of lawful behaviour are beginning to break down. I think the author also gives us the sad image of a mother being dependant on the eyes (and judgement) of her very young child. When asked whether her child can see she says she can but immediately adds 'But I can't.' The mother is in a very difficult position and the author does not want us to judge her for what she does. (4)

Level 2 (The Day of the Triffids)

1. It is quiet with a great sense of everything having changed. The sound of the tapping getting louder and coming closer, at first unidentified, adds tension until the narrator (and the reader) realise what it is. (3)

2. He makes it clear that suddenly to be 'normally blind' is a reassuring advantage rather than a handicap. Vehicles have been abandoned (so the inference is that no one can see to drive) so that everything is quiet: a point reinforced by the description of the blind man tapping along which wouldn't normally be heard. He uses words such as 'groping' and 'collisions' to emphasise the fact that people trying to move about are likely to walk into each other. No one can get food in the conventional way so the ordinary rules of lawful behaviour are beginning to break down. The author shows us an otherwise apparently respectable, well-dressed man breaking a shop window to steal fruit. The author also presents us with the sad image of a mother being dependant on the eyes (and judgement) of her very young child – a poignant role reversal. (4)

3. The man has the qualities of jauntiness and confidence because he knows from long experience how to get about. Once he is told what has happened, and he has thought about it, he seems rather pleased – giving a 'short bitter laugh'– because he is now the one with the advantages. We are told that he walks away from the narrator 'with an exaggerated air of independence' and 'a little defiantly' which stresses his newfound cheerfulness. He has evidently resented being a victim of charity and sympathy in the past – as shown by his bitterness – and is now delighted that the rest of the population will need its 'patronage' for itself. (6)

4. The 'woman who carried a small child' reminds the reader how difficult the situation is for ordinary people. The woman cannot see and they need food. This is a horrifying predicament. Second, Mary, the little girl, is very young. She whines, has to be carried and speaks childishly. Yet the child can see and the mother can't. The mother understands this but the child evidently does not and the reader feels sympathy. Third, we can see, too, that this child is going to be very valuable, not just to her mother but maybe also to others, which will make her vulnerable. That is why the author presents the man they collide with who immediately uses the child's eyes to help him find food ('Look, Sonny, what's in there?') and although he shares it with the woman and child, others might not. (6)

5. The author shows us what his five characters are like through what they say in this passage. We hear the exasperated – and slightly puzzled – self-reliance of the 'normally blind' man when he says to the narrator 'I've already been bumped into by God knows how many fools today.' He speaks assertively and almost angrily because he is used to being patronised, but he parts from the narrator fairly politely. Although this incident is slightly comic it also draws attention to the frightening strangeness which surrounds everybody in the passage. The conversation between 'the young man in the well-cut suit' and the mother and child makes us realise how desperate they are. All three are hungry. None would normally steal ('We didn't ought to take 'em. Not like this' says the woman) but the young man is able to rationalise and persuade: 'How else are you going to get food?' The author uses speech in this passage to show us that these people come from different social classes. The woman and her child speak with a local accent in contrast to the young man who speaks to them. This reminds us that the disaster is affecting nearly everyone equally and breaking down barriers between groups. Dialogue also makes the action move faster and more incisively – like a play. These characters answer each other quickly and that too helps to reinforce their feeling of helplessness at the horrifying situation they find themselves in.   (6)

2. Travel writing

Level 1 (Under the Tuscan Sun)

1. (a) She likes the way they are shaped like twisted letters (hieroglyphics). She admires their ability to navigate by the stars even when indoors.   (2)

    (b) The tools in the outhouses interest her because they show how life was in the past.   (2)

2. 'usual homes in dusty corners' and 'I trap them in a jar and take them outside.'   (2)

    The writer is comfortable with nature and interested in it. She regards the house as the scorpions' home as well as hers. It is a tolerant attitude.

    Rather than being frightened of the scorpions in her house and trying aggressively to get rid of them she observes them closely. She respectfully traps the creatures in a jar and takes them outside rather than killing them and seems quite sorry if she accidentally sucks some into the vacuum cleaner.   (4)

3. The writer and her husband are foreigners as she makes clear. The local people, who 'pause in the road and look up at all the mad activity' would probably find it odd that these Americans want to live in this old house which needs so much work doing to it. They pass by and try to strike up conversations because they're curious and Mayes conveys this by mentioning them and including some of what they say. Second, she imagines them thinking about 'the car trunk full of bottles, mattress flying, me screaming as a scorpion falls down my shirt when I sweep the stone walls of the stall, Ed wielding a grim-reaper scythe through the weeds.' Local people would, she speculates, be amused by such activity.   (4)

4. 'rusted pans, newspapers from 1958, wire, paint cans, debris' and 'as parched as the hills around us'. (2)

    I have chosen these two quotations because they are different from each other. The first reminds us that the house Mayes is trying to make habitable is full of rubbish and it is very hard work to clear it out. She is also operating in a very hot dry place with very little rainfall. She and Ed are thirsty just as the surrounding hills are dry and dusty. (4)

5. She tells us that she used to use an American cookware shop. Now she cooks pasta with wooden spoons and a few other very basic kitchen tools. They are very busy and active – becoming dry and thirsty, 'as parched as the hills around us'. They are gently modernising the kitchen – with a new fridge and stove – but have adapted to the fairly primitive arrangements for hot water which has to be carried by hand from the bathroom and having to make do with an improvised kitchen work surface. They are working so hard and for so long each day that they sleep well and have very healthy appetites. She tells us about the simple, but very appealing, food they cook to show how contented they are. For example: they eat lots of local olives, pasta, tomato and mozzarella salad and green salads made from wild arugula. Before they came to this place they would have lived differently. (5)

Level 2 (Under the Tuscan Sun)

1. She enjoys the way they are shaped like twisted letters (hieroglyphics). She admires their ability to navigate by the stars even when indoors. (2)

2. The tools in the outhouses show how life was in the past. One is a tool for trimming grapes. Another is an old-fashioned container for hot coals for warming beds on damp, cold nights. (2)

3. The writer, who admires 'the beauty of scorpions', is comfortable with nature and interested in it. Rather than being frightened of the minibeasts in her house and trying aggressively to get rid of them she observes them closely. She respectfully traps the scorpions in a jar and takes them outside rather than killing them and seems quite sorry if she accidentally sucks some into the vacuum cleaner. Even the scorpion in the bidet or the white one from her pillow doesn't faze her much. Second she notices 'Whole eco-sytems of spiders and scorpions' in her house but doesn't seem to mind that they come straight back when she tries to get rid of them. (4)

4. The writer and her husband are foreigners. The local people 'pause in the road and look up at all the mad activity' because they find it odd that that Mayes and Ed should want to live in this old house which needs so much work doing to it. Neighbours pass by and try to strike up conversations because they're curious. Mayes conveys this by mentioning them and including some of what they say. Second, to the locals, the two 'incomers' would have seemed very eccentric and Mayes sees things from the onlookers' point of view with her description: 'the car trunk full of bottles, mattress flying, me screaming as a scorpion falls down my shirt when I sweep the stone walls of the stall, Ed wielding a grim-reaper scythe through the weeds.' The cultural differences are there too. She is surprised at the casual enquiry about the house price from complete strangers. (4)

5.   Mayes contrasts shopping in a fancy American cookware shop, 'Williams-Sonoma' which, in America she treats as a 'toy store' with the simplicity of cooking pasta with wooden spoons and a few other very basic kitchen tools in her 'surprisingly manageable kitchen' despite its lack of modern fittings and running hot water. She has even grown used to bringing 'hot water from the bathroom in a plastic laundry pan'. Second, she remembers seeing the house before they bought it full of 'fanciful iron beds with painted medallions of Mary and shepherds holding lambs, wormy chests of drawers with marble tops, cribs, foxed mirrors, cradles, boxes, and lugubrious bleeding-heart religious pictures of the Crucifixion' but now, in stark contrast, it contains only scorpions, spiders and rubbish.   (6)

6.   They are very busy and physically active – becoming dry and thirsty, 'as parched as the hills around us.' They are gently modernising the kitchen – with a new fridge and stove – but have adapted to the fairly primitive arrangements for hot water which has to be carried by hand from the bathroom. They are happy to make do with an improvised kitchen work surface consisting of a trestle arrangement and the basic implements for cooking. Because they are working so hard – 'we haul and scrub' – and for so long each day they sleep well and have very healthy appetites. 'After long work, we eat everything in sight then tumble like field hands into bed,' she says. We infer, because she's telling us all this, that their lives, activity levels and diet in America would have been very different.   (7)

3. Biography/autobiography

Level 1 (Anita and Me)

1.   When she's not at work (and wearing 'sensible teacher's trouser suits') the writer's mother likes to dress in traditional style. She wears silk saris and 'discreet gold jewellery'.   (2)

   She does this because she wants to show English people that Indian women can look elegant and tasteful without resembling 'ambulating Christmas trees'.   (2)

2.   The writer understands why her mother feels as she does about tasteful clothes and the 'ability to speak English without an accent'. But she finds it irritating. She comments, with irony, that her mother seemed to regard it as her 'duty' to provide 'English people's education'. The writer suggests, with exasperation ('but for her') that her mother would get 'fewer stares and whispers' had she worn ordinary British clothes which the writer would presumably have preferred when they are out together. All this seems to point to disagreement between the writer and her mother.   (4)

3.   There is tension between the writer's parents. Something is upsetting her mother who is 'quiet now, no light in her face'. That is why her father is trying to cheer her up with a meringue and he seems to be on edge because he snaps at his daughter when she chips in unhelpfully with a pert comment about her mother's attitude to shop-bought food: 'You know what she will say. I can make this cheaper at home.' In the car the parents quietly discuss in 'soft whispers' some troubling secret they are not sharing with their daughter. The mother seems 'to wipe something from her face' so she is in tears and her husband is watching her anxiously in the mirror as he drives – observed by his daughter in the back. (5)

4.   The writer who is clearly fond of food ('the spongy belly of my rum baba', 'licking the tomato sauce') gets a piece of sausage stuck in her throat. She makes it funny by pretending, in an exaggerated way, that it is a tragic drama although really it is just a bit of sausage. She uses words like 'thrilled' and 'dramatic' which are deliberately unsuitable here. There is also a witty anti-climax in her earnest desire to write about her plight on the windscreen to attract attention before realising that she 'could not spell sausage'. There is comedy too in the fact that the parents are dealing with some adult drama of their own and unaware that, in the back, their daughter might be choking to death on something as ordinary and undignified as a piece of sausage.   (6)

5.   The writer is growing up in Britain and finding some difficulty with her parents' Indian ways such as her mother's determination to look 'glamorous in saris' to show English people how it can be done. She would prefer her mother to dress as British people do in one of 'her sensible teacher's trouser suits'. The author wants to conform.

That seems also be why she likes British junk food (rum babas and hot dogs) rather than anything Indian. Her father buys her the hot dog as an apology for snapping at her (and to shut her up?) so he clearly knows that this is the sort of thing she likes.

She is very observant and her descriptive language underlines this: 'my mother's bracelets jingled', 'vibrating thin silks'. She contrasts the other Indian women they see in Birmingham, for instance, in their brightly coloured traditional clothes, 'screaming with greens and pinks and yellows', with her mother's gentle clothes and imagines the other women justifying their 'incongruous' woollen socks and cardigans by saying 'damn cold country'.

She presents herself as a selfish child who is thinking more about her birthday and what she is given to eat – 'they were leaving me out again'– rather than thinking about what might be troubling her mother.   (6)

Level 2 (Anita and Me)

1.   (a) She is an educated woman (a teacher) and wants to give an impression of Indian women which helps to make British people see them as acceptable. For her, that means wearing traditional Indian dress elegantly without looking gaudy.   (2)

     (b) The writer is impatient with this view and thinks her mother would do better to wear the ordinary British clothes she wears to school. There is a note of exasperated sarcasm in her observation that her mother sees 'English people's education' as 'her duty'.   (2)

2.   In the tense scene in the café the writer gives a humorous account of her younger self tucking cheerfully into a rum baba (it's her birthday) while her mother refuses to eat anything. The writer makes it clear that at the time she doesn't really know what is upsetting her mother who is unusually quiet, but she is irritated by her mother's refusal to join in by having a cake. The tension is suggested in the contrast between the writer's enjoyment of her cake and her mother's attitude to eating out. We don't hear the mother speak in this passage which helps to evoke a sense of her being upset and her daughter's being impervious to it. The narrator assumes – and rudely spells it out – that her mother objects to paying for an expensive, inferior shop-bought cake and trots out some of her

mother's usual arguments. We infer from this that the writer is often told by her mother that English food is overpriced and unpleasant and that she can make better at home. The writer, who is eating an ordinary British cake, clearly finds this infuriating and would simply like to conform to British ways. (4)

3. The writer's father is concerned about his wife who seems to be upset ('no light in her face') and is being kind to her in the café by trying to persuade her to have something to eat that he knows she likes – a meringue. He seems to be kind and loving. Second, we also see him very angry with his daughter because of her rude outburst against her mother – from which we can deduce that he and his wife have a strong supportive relationship. But then the mother silently asks the father not to be so hard on his daughter by covering the child's hand and shaking her head at her husband. It is clear that the couple are well attuned to each other. Third, once the three of them are in the car he and his wife talk to each other softly and exclude their daughter. The word 'again' is significant. The writer makes it clear that there is some ongoing issue which she doesn't, child as she is, understand. It is obvious too that the mother is in tears ('seemed to wipe something from her face') in the front of the car, although her daughter is oblivious. (5)

4. The final paragraph includes words such as 'squeezed', 'shot' and 'lodged', which are witty overstatements in this context so it is comic.

    The writer's father has bought her a compensatory hot dog because it's her birthday and, gently reprimanded by his wife, he regrets telling her off. When a piece of sausage gets stuck in her throat she briefly thinks she's going to die – which seems glamorous and exciting. 'I felt thrilled. It was so dramatic,' she says.

    The contrast to the glamour comes as a comic anti-climax. She can't get the attention of her preoccupied parents because she 'could not spell sausage'.

    Set against this is the anxious, whispered conversation ('They were still talking, engrossed') going on between her impervious parents in the front of the car. Something serious is distressing them and that heightens the situation comedy of their daughter in the back choking on something as mundane as a lump of sausage. (6)

5. The writer – an adult looking back, obviously – recalls and presents herself as a rather self-absorbed child. She is annoyed that on her birthday her parents are preoccupied about something else and 'they were leaving me out again'. The irritation and frustration with her mother is clearly ongoing. The mother says none of the things attributed to her while the family is in the café. The writer is regurgitating what she so often hears her mother say.

    She is clearly keen on food. She evokes the exact consistency of the rum baba's 'spongy belly' and we can almost taste the tomato sauce on the hot dog and hear her singing (to draw attention from her parents?) 'between slurps'. On the other hand, she is aware that her mother is upset although she chooses to ignore it. She notices her father's eyes anxiously flicking towards his wife while he is driving, having also seen, but not apparently recognised, her mother shedding a tear. The adult narrator wants us to see 'past' her child self and work out with her, as readers, what was really going on. The writer is also a humorist and, with hindsight, can see the funny side of the events she's remembering. (6)

4. Drama

Level 1 (War Horse)

1. Nicholls wants Joey to get used to the sound of gunfire so that he won't panic
    in battle.   (1)

    Joey 'reacts' to each shot but is probably gradually taking less notice of them.
    He presumably jumps and has to be comforted by Nicholls. This is a stage direction
    and exactly what happens here would need to be worked out between the director
    and cast.   (1)

2. Nicholls doesn't want his men to have anything shiny on their bodies which might
    glint in the sun and attract enemy attention.   (1)

    Ned seems surprised or even annoyed because of all the work he has done in the
    past. From Nicholl's comment 'I know, Warren, after all that hard work' we gather that
    he sees some sort of irritation in Warren's face.   (2)

3. 'Two proud animals' and 'Joey and Topthorn are only interested in each other.' (2)

    'Two proud animals' tells us that these horses have dignity and personality but they don't
    yet know each other very well and seem a bit wary of each other or 'snippy'.

    'The two horses are only interested in each other' comes after the horses have been seen
    reacting to each other in a paddock. They seem to be forming some sort of bond and
    working out how to relate to each other.   (2)

4. Stewart is partly excited and partly nervous. He wants to 'cut a swathe through Fritz'
    but he is also thinking about stories he's heard from his uncle. He has been told that
    the men – the enemy – sometimes fall apart when they see a British cavalry charge.
    He speaks with courage and bravado but there's also a sense that he doesn't really
    know what to expect.   (3)

5. These men hold different army ranks. Nicholls is evidently the most senior – he gives the
    orders and stops Stewart from thinking too much about the stories his uncle has told him.
    Stewart is a captain in charge of a troop which Nicholls asks him about. He has not been
    into battle before. Ned is a trooper and perhaps younger. He just takes instructions and
    doesn't speak other than to acknowledge orders.   (6)

6. 'warlike and violent' and 'men tend to go to pieces'   (2)

    Everyone in this scene is feeling tense because they are thinking about what they face
    tomorrow when they will have to be 'warlike and violent'. It sums up the nervousness and
    fear they are all feeling. Nicholls is reflecting on the calm, peaceful horses and imagining a
    nightmare world in which they too become violent like men.

    All of them know, without spelling it out, that 'men tend to go to pieces' in battle –
    whichever side they are on – although Stewart applies it only to the Germans here.
    It underlines the terror they are dealing with and the horror they face. They have to be
    brave, obviously, but thinking about it is making them tense. Stewart talks of how they will
    'cut a swathe through Fritz' although, as Nicholls tells him, he will have to find
    out for himself just what it's like to be in a battle.   (5)

Level 2 (War Horse)

1. Nicholls is getting Joey used to very loud, close noise and to the smell of cordite so that when he is in battle he won't panic. (1)

   The noise of the guns clearly needs to be very loud so there should be no other sound. The people puppeting Joey should make him jump and flinch but less for each gun shot as he gradually becomes 'desensitised'. (2)

2. Nicholls doesn't want his men to have anything shiny on their bodies which might glint in the sun and attract enemy attention. (1)

   He says 'I know, Warren, after all that hard work' which suggests that Ned looks surprised, or even annoyed, because soldiers are normally expected to spend a lot of time polishing their boots, buckles and other equipment. (2)

3. Joey is the horse Nicholls is working with while Captain Stewart is using Topthorn. Both are 'proud animals'. Joey seems to be slightly faster when they practise charging because Nicholls gently ribs the captain about being behind and Stewart says 'We were breathing right down your neck, as you well know.' The two horses are interested in each other – when they are brought together at the end of the scene they make that clear although they evidently don't yet know each other well. Stewart tells Nicholls that they are 'snippy' with each other, which from the context seems to mean 'wary' and trying to work out which of them is dominant. (4)

4. Stewart is partly excited and partly nervous. He wants to 'cut a swathe through Fritz' by which he means to attack the Germans and beat them. He is also thinking about stories he's heard from his uncle who says that 'men tend to go to pieces when our cavalry bear down on them.' So he believes that men – the enemy – sometimes fall apart when they see a British cavalry charge. He speaks with courage and bravado but there's also a sense that he doesn't really know what to expect. We get a sense that Stewart's feelings are mixed. (4)

5. The playwright makes it clear that these men hold different army ranks. He uses speech, action and silence to make the differences clear.

   Nicholls is evidently the most senior – he is shown giving the orders and takes charge of the conversation very assertively in response to Stewart's reference to his uncle: 'every generation has to discover things for themselves' he says firmly (but ungrammatically). He is also courteous and respectful: 'not casting aspersions on your uncle's experience'.

   Stewart is a lower-ranking officer, a captain – the playwright has Nicholls ask him about his troop to make this clear. We infer that, unlike Nicholls, he has not been into battle before because he is speculating about the expected conflict the next day. The playwright shows him talking excitedly and in garrulous detail about what he hopes to do to the Germans: 'he won't know what's hit him. He'll wish he'd never been born' which is the playwright's way of showing Stewart's nervousness.

   Ned is not an officer but a trooper and may be younger (the playwright uses his first name). He takes instructions about practical things such as polishing and doesn't speak other than to acknowledge orders. He says very little but his function here is to remind the reader/theatre audience that as well as officers such as Stewart and Nicholls there are many thousands of ordinary men, many of them very young like Ned. (5)

6. None of these men should seem at all relaxed. All their thoughts are focused on what they will face when they arrive in France to 'put a swathe through Fritz'. The 'rapid rounds' being fired near Joey at the beginning should be against a background of quiet. Just as Joey reacts, so should the audience.

The actors, now it is clear that they're 'posted to France' should show their tension in their movements, perhaps by pacing about, clenching their hands or drumming their fingers, although each is desperate not to show the others how tense he is feeling.

Nicholls speaks gently to Joey: 'Good boy. This is a gun. The smell is cordite. Try again.' He has to appear calm to Ned and Stewart because he is the most senior, but the actor should make us sense that beneath the surface he is apprehensive when he says, for example 'I was pleased with the practice charge today.' Unlike Stewart, and presumably Ned, Nicholls has experienced frontline war before so has more reason to be frightened than the others, although they too are nervous. And the horses will sense this so the puppeteers manipulating them should make the animals jumpy too. (6)

7.2 Chapter 3

Level 1 (Sunken Evening)

1. The starlings are flying in and out of the hollows and spaces in the walls of the church, 'stowing' bits and pieces. Gradually the movement stops, the church 'settles' and because it is evening we infer the birds do too. There had been bird movement around the church. Now there is not. Everything is still and quiet. (1)

2. The typist has to stay at her desk because she must answer the telephone. All she can see is bubbles which symbolise something very fragile (possibly freedom) which soon disappears. (2)

The poet is comparing himself with an oyster. He sees himself as having a hard, grey, crusty shell, but with something precious – the poem – inside, like an oyster's pearl. (2)

3. 'feathered fish' and 'sandy grottoes' (2)

The whole poem is a metaphor in which the poet compares the city with the sea. The 'feathered fish' which are really birds, sound delicate because of the alliteration. They are part of the metaphor. So are the 'sandy grottoes' in a nearby wide road away from the deepest water. The poet is comparing the spacious openness of the roads with big caves. (4)

4. In the last verse it is completely dark and time for workers to go home. The poet imagines the tide going out as the city empties so that the workers are washed with the tide and stranded in their suburbs. Night, which 'trawls its heavy net', is personified as a fisherman dragging the workers like fish through shallow waters towards their homes on the outskirts of the city. (4)

5.	'The Mall', 'the fountains' silver weed' and 'hauls the clerk to Surbiton'	(2)

The poet is imagining a big city where lots of people, who live on the outskirts, travel to work and home again in the evening. It has a large square with fountains where starlings and pigeons settle and a road called 'the Mall'. Some of the commuters live in a suburb called Surbiton.	(3)

Note: The poet is actually imagining the Trafalgar Square area of London. He mentions 'the Mall' which feeds into Trafalgar Square and the 'fountains' silver weed' could be the fountains in the square. This is also a famous spot for pigeons and starlings. We can be sure this is London rather than some other city because Surbiton is a London suburb.

6.	Darkness fell and I left my office and set off to the bus-stop along with hundreds of others with the twittering of roosting starlings and sparrows around us in the damp. We swept along the street like a wave, most of us pretty tired and desperate to get home after a long day's work. Once on the crawling lobster-red bus, the journey took a long time because of the traffic, but as we got farther away from the city centre it began to thin out – like coming to the surface after a long underwater swim. Getting home at last was peaceful and a great relief.	(5)

Level 2 (Sunken Evening)

1.	The starlings are flying in and out of the hollows and spaces in the walls of the church, carrying bits and pieces. The poet imagines them bringing metaphorical mussel shells to a wreck as if the birds were underwater creatures. Their feathers have a multi-coloured sheen which reminds the poet of the shiny phosphorescence sometimes seen on the surface of the sea.	(3)

2.	The whole poem is an extended metaphor in which the poet compares the city with the sea. Because the light is green it is like an underwater scene. In this metaphor the birds are 'feathered fish' (a good expression because of the alliteration which makes them sound very light). The slow (red) buses are compared with lobsters and the blue-ish grey pigeons with prawns. The fountains in the square, with their spraying water, look like waterweed and the wide road nearby has 'sandy grottoes'. The church is described as a wreck (perhaps it was damaged – maybe in a war) with a long shape which resembles the hull of a ship.	(4)

3.	The typist has to stay at her desk because she must answer the telephone. It is as if she were trapped on the sea bed so she gazes longingly toward the surface of the water and the sky because that would be freedom. All she can see is bubbles which symbolise something very fragile which soon disappears. The poet is comparing himself with an unattractive looking oyster with a hard grey crusty shell but with something precious and beautiful – the poem – inside, like an oyster's pearl.	(4)

4.	The last verse hangs on its first word – the adverb 'Till' – which is a turning point to show that the poem is about to move off in a different direction. It is now dark and time for the workers to go home.	(1)

The poet imagines the tide going out as the city empties so that the workers are washed out of the deep sea and stranded. Night, which 'trawls its heavy net', is personified as a fisherman dragging the workers like fish through shallow waters towards their homes on the outskirts of the city. They are then stranded by the tide in their suburbs. (2)

5.   The poet is imagining a big city where lots of people, who live on the outskirts, travel to work and home again in the evening. It has a 'city square' with fountains where starlings and pigeons are and there is a road called 'the Mall'. Some of the commuters live in a suburb called 'Surbiton'. (6)

Note: The poet is actually imagining the Trafalgar Square area of London. He mentions 'the Mall' which feeds into Trafalgar Square and the 'fountains' silver weed' could be the fountains in the square. This is a famous spot for pigeons and starlings and there is a church – St Martin-in-the-Fields – on one side of the square. We can be sure this is London rather than some other city because Surbiton is a London suburb.

6.   This poem presents London at dusk and compares its emptying and gradual quietening with the tide going out. Verbs such as 'floods' and trawls' and nouns such as 'squalls', 'weed' and 'bubbles' help to sustain the metaphor which runs right through the poem to create an imaginative picture. The poet's rhyme scheme in each stanza, uses half ('fish'/'splash,' 'run'/'Surbiton') as well as full rhymes ('dry'/'sky', 'fret'/'net') which gives the poem a fluid feel which complements the marine imagery. The occasional use of internal rhyme within stanzas ('trawls'/'hauls', 'bell'/ 'shells') adds to this effect. So does the use of alliteration in, for example, 'fowl and feathered fish', 'typist, trapped by telephones'. The rhythm evokes the idea of waves and the tide. The poet mixes polysyllables with monosyllables ('phosphorescent starlings', 'tide and fret') to build the rhythm of moving water. Overall I find this quite moving poem makes successful use of many techniques which, together, form a satisfying and imaginative description of London at twilight. (5)

7.3 Chapter 6

Test yourself

1.   A noun is a naming word.

2.   A verb is an action or 'being' word.

3.   An adjective is a describing word which qualifies or modifies a noun.

4.   An adverb is a describing word which qualifies or modifies a verb.

5.   A pronoun stands in the place of a noun.

6.   A preposition tells you the position of something in relation to something else.

7.   A conjunction is a joining word.

8.   A full stop, question mark or exclamation mark can end a sentence.

9.   Speech marks are sometimes called inverted commas or quotation marks.

10. It's a great shame that the tree has lost its leaves as it's Dad's favourite.